Say NO to Summer Slide and YES to Summer Smart!

Parents, you know that for kids, summer always seems to fly by without a care in the world (and hey—they deserve the break!). But research shows that if kids stop learning entirely over summer vacation, they can lose up to 2½ months' worth of knowledge from the previous grade through "summer learning loss." That's why we at Sylvan created the **Summer Smart Workbook** series!

By adding just a few pages per day into kids' summer routines, you can help your child keep their skills fresh and set them up for 2nd grade academic success in the fall. Our **Summer Smart** workbooks bring you:

- Over 100 colorful pages of **fun, teacher-created learning exercises** that reinforce reading and math skills

- **Recommended summer book lists** (for both reading *and* math topics—yes, there are fun math books out there!), plus discussion questions to spark comprehension

- A **Vacation Challenge section full of bonus games and activities** that take learning off the page and into the real world

- Bonus **cut-out flashcards** to use for learning on the go

- A **"Summer Smart!" Achievement Certificate** you can display once your child has completed the workbook

Your child will love the great mix of activities, stories, and games in these pages. *You'll* love seeing their improved confidence and newfound love of learning. With **Sylvan Summer Smart**, you don't have to compromise between entertainment and education—instead, you can get a jump-start on making school a positive experience in the fall!

Thanks for choosing us to help foster the development of confident, well-prepared, independent learners!

The Sylvan Team

Here's what some families have shared about Sylvan workbooks:

"Using Sylvan workbooks helps my child keep an interest in school subjects while not in school. It helps keep his focus on the importance of learning even when outside his school environment. And it also helps me during those interminable 'I'm bored' days!" – *B.B. Lawson*

"My daughter has improved her academic skills and confidence while completing Sylvan workbooks. She also was excited to complete the Sylvan workbook pages, because they are engaging but challenging at the same time. She is looking forward to completing more pages throughout the summer to keep her skills up. Thank you, Sylvan, for this!" – *K. Haynes*

"[They] often include games and puzzles that are creative and educational, which helped my son, who doesn't like to study, brush up on skills, and even learn past his grade level! Sylvan is now part of my son's daily routine and eases up pressure and dependence on parents too." – *F. Mohamed*

Connect with your local Sylvan Learning Center and make an even bigger impact this summer!

Every child has the ability to learn, but sometimes children need help making it happen. Sylvan Learning uses a proven, personalized approach to building and mastering the learning skills needed to unlock your child's potential. Our in-center programs deliver unparalleled results that other supplemental education services simply can't match.

To learn more about Sylvan and our innovative in-center programs, call 1-800-EDUCATE or visit www.SylvanLearning.com. *With over 750 locations in North America, there's a Sylvan Learning Center near you!*

Summer Smart
Between Grades 1 & 2

This book belongs to

_____

Published in the United States by Random House, Inc., New York, and in Canada by Random House of Canada Limited, Toronto.

A Penguin Random House Company.

The material in this workbook was previously published in *1st Grade Reading Skill Builders* and *1st Grade Math Games & Puzzles* as trade paperbacks in 2009 and 2010, and as *1st Grade Spelling Flashcards* and *1st Grade Math Flashcards* in 2011 and 2013 by Sylvan Learning, Inc., an imprint of Penguin Random House, LLC.

www.sylvanlearning.com

Cover Design: Suzanne Lee
Summer Smart Interior Production: Big Yellow Taxi, Inc.

Original Workbook Credits:
Producer & Editorial Direction: The Linguistic Edge
Producer: TJ Trochlil McGreevy
Writers: Christina Roll and Amy Kraft
Cover and Interior Illustrations: Tim Goldman and Duendes del Sur
Layout and Art Direction: SunDried Penguin
Art Manager: Adina Ficano

First Edition

ISBN: 978-0-525-56918-3
ISSN: 2639-8273

This book is available at special discounts for bulk purchases for sales promotions or premiums. For more information, write to Special Markets/Premium Sales, 1745 Broadway, MD 6-2, New York, New York 10019 or e-mail specialmarkets@randomhouse.com.

PRINTED IN THE UNITED STATES OF AMERICA

10 9 8 7 6 5 4 3

Contents

Contents

Section 1:
Summer Smart Reading

Starting Line

SAY the name of each picture and LISTEN to its beginning sound. WRITE the letter to complete each word. Then READ each word out loud.

ike
1

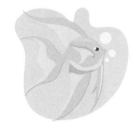
ed
2

ish
3

oat
4

og
5

esk
6

us
7

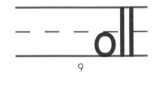
ork
8

oll
9

um
10

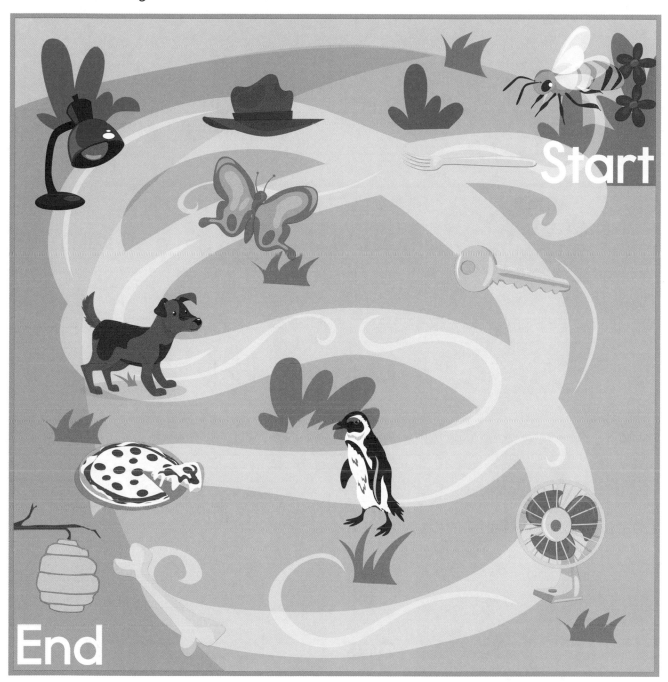

Maze Crazy!

Help the bee get to the hive. DRAW a line through the maze to connect the pictures whose names begin with the **b**, **d**, or **f** sound.

1

Sounds and Words

SAY the name of the picture in each row and LISTEN to its beginning sound. CIRCLE the word or words in the row that have the same beginning sound.

1.  quick   quit   fun

2.  jeans   gum   jam

3.  kite   kick   goat

4.  mop   fan   hand

5.  gas   keep   zip

What's My Word?

SAY the name of each picture. CIRCLE the word that matches the picture.

1.

hand   jam

2.

rang   king

3.

queen   nail

4.

jump   jar

5.

kite   tent

6.

girl   quilt

7.

hat   fall

8.

jug   key

Beginning Sounds

What Starts My Name?

SAY the name of each picture. WRITE the correct word for each picture under the letter that makes its beginning sound. LOOK at the word box for help.

leaf	net	pan	mop	pig	log	mat	~~nose~~

l   **m**   **n**   **p**

nose

Picture Match

READ each sentence and FIND the matching picture. WRITE the correct number in the box.

1. I see a ladybug on a leaf.

2. The milk is on the mat.

3. The nest is next to the net.

4. I ate pizza and pie for lunch.

Beginning Sounds

Starting Line

SAY the name of each picture and LISTEN to its beginning sound. WRITE the letter to complete each word. Then READ each word out loud.

___ent
1

___ing
2

___ooth
3

___ooster
4

___omato
5

___eal
6

6
___ix
7

___ed
8

___ub
9

___aw
10

Double Cross

SAY the name of each picture and LISTEN to its beginning sound. DRAW a line from each picture to its name.

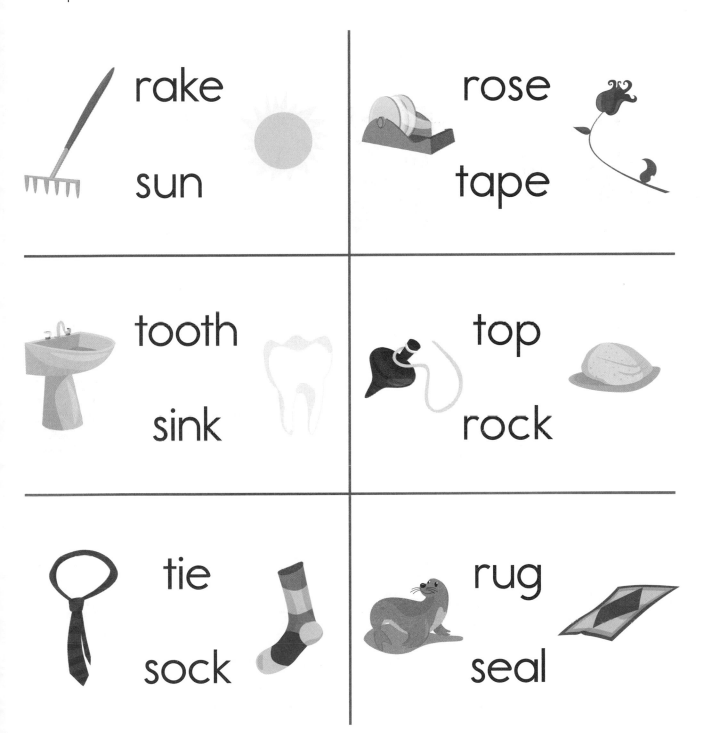

rake

sun

rose

tape

tooth

sink

top

rock

tie

sock

rug

seal

Beginning Sounds

What Starts My Name?

SAY the name of each picture. WRITE the correct word for each picture under the letter that makes its beginning sound. LOOK at the word box for help.

| zipper | van | wig | yo-yo | web | yellow | vase | zebra |

V   W   y   z

_____   _____   _____   _____

_____   _____   _____   _____

_____   _____   _____   _____

Word Connection

SAY the name of the picture. CIRCLE the letters that make its name. WRITE the word. Then READ the word out loud.

ⓥet
cⓐⓝ

_____
ˉv̲a̲n̲ˉ
1

m e s b
v u p t

_____
_____
2

w i m f
t o n g

_____
_____
3

x- l a y
h r u p

_____
_____
4

g e r n
y a m c

_____
_____
5

z e p u
s i r o

_____
_____
6

11

2

Finish Line

SAY the name of each picture and LISTEN to its ending sound. WRITE the letter to complete each word. Then READ each word out loud.

re ___
1

han ___
6

su ___
2

cri ___
7

mo ___
3

ra ___
8

dru ___
4

to ___
9

fa ___
5

moo ___
10

Circle It

SAY the name of the picture in each row. CIRCLE the word or words in the row that have the same ending sound.

1. gum   bird   clam

2. seed   moon   log

3. food   sad   wig

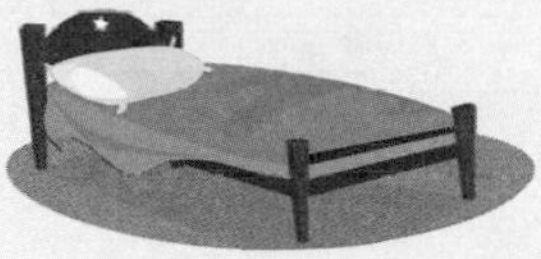

4. jump   hook   top

5. fix   rub   jet

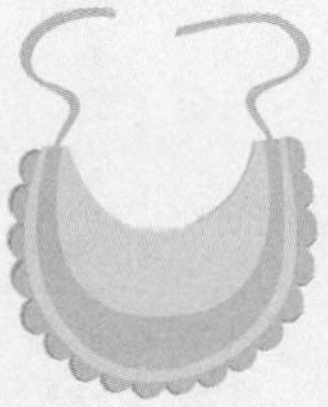

Word Connection

SAY the name of the picture. CIRCLE the letters that make its name. WRITE the word. Then READ the word out loud.

g e a k
b o e t

_____
- - - - -
_____
1

b a s l
f e l s

_____
- - - - -
_____
2

s h a g
f l i p

_____
- - - - -
_____
3

p r e t t
d l a s s

_____
- - - - -
_____
4

f a r n
b o r k

_____
- - - - -
_____
5

Double Cross

SAY the name of each picture and LISTEN to its ending sound. DRAW a line from each picture to its name.

nut

bag

nail

duck

bus

net

shell

clock

gift

doll

gas

pig

Stuck in the Middle

SAY the name of each picture and LISTEN to its middle sound. WRITE the letter or letters to complete each word. Then READ each word out loud.

HINT: You may need to add more than one letter to some words.

 mi __ en
₁

 ro __ ot
6

 se __ en
2

 le __ on
7

 pi __ ow
3

ki __ en
8

 pi __ a
4

 la __ er
9

 zi __ er
5

 ra __ oon
10

Circle It

SAY the name of the picture in each row and LISTEN to its middle sound. CIRCLE the word or words in the row that have the same middle sound.

1. pepper   metal   carrot

2.  jacket   dinner   lizard

3.  spider   wizard   hammer

4. muffin   ticket   jelly

5.  parrot   wagon   chicken

Starting Line

SAY the name of each picture and LISTEN to its beginning sound. WRITE the letters to complete each word. Then READ each word out loud.

umb
1

uck
2

air
3

oe
4

irt
5

ip
6

ark
7

ee
8

imble
9

eese
10

Blank Out

READ each sentence and LOOK at the picture. WRITE the word to complete the sentence. LOOK at the word box for help.

brush	beach	splash	moth	bench

The whale made a big _____ .
1

A _____ is on the rose.
2

The shell is on the _____ .
3

The _____ is on the easel.
4

A man is sitting on the _____ .
5

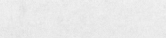

5 Same Sound

The word *hat* has a short **a** in the middle.

SAY the name for each picture. WRITE "a" if you hear the short **a** sound.

Maze Crazy!

Help the ram find the flag. DRAW a line through the maze to connect the pictures whose names have the short **a** sound.

Match and Write

The word *hen* has a short **e** in the middle.

SAY the name for each picture. FIND the correct name in the word box and CIRCLE it. Then WRITE the word.

| web | nest | pen | net | sled | bed |

1

2

3

4

5

6

What Am I?

WRITE the answers in the blanks. The words have the same vowel sound as in the word *hen*.

I am a bird's home.

_____
1

I am what a
hen lays.

_____
2

I am the number that
comes after nine.

10

_____
3

I am what a spider
spins.

_____
4

I am what you
sleep in.

_____
5

5

Match Up

The word *wig* has a short **i** in the middle.

READ and TRACE each word. DRAW a line from the word to its matching picture.

pig

bib

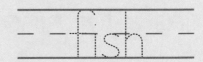
fish

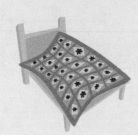

pin

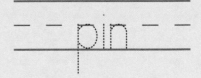
quilt

Time to Rhyme

SAY the name of each picture. CIRCLE the word or words that rhyme.

1.   hush   dish   wish

2.   pat   map   pit

3.   bib   sip   let

4.   big   peg   wig

5.   sit   mix   sack

Same Sound

The word *dog* has a short **o** in the middle.

SAY the name for each picture. WRITE "o" if you hear the short **o** sound.

Maze Crazy!

Help the frog leap to the rock. DRAW a line through the maze to connect the pictures whose names have the short **o** sound.

Match and Write

The word *cup* has a short **u** sound in the middle.

SAY the name for each picture. FIND the correct name in the word box and CIRCLE it. Then WRITE the word.

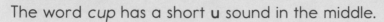

| bus | mud | tub | plug | sun | rug |

1

2

3

4

5

6

Blank Out

READ each sentence. LOOK at the picture. WRITE the word to complete the sentence. LOOK at the word box for help.

cup	sub	gum	rug	truck

The bug is on the _____.
1

The pup is as small as a _____.
2

The _____ is in the sun.
3

It's fun to chew _____.
4

The _____ is stuck in the mud.
5

6

Same Sound

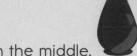

The word *vase* has a long **a** sound in the middle.

SAY the name for each picture. WRITE "a" if you hear the long **a** sound.

Maze Crazy!

Help the snake get to the gate. DRAW a line through the maze, connecting the pictures whose names have the long **a** sound.

6

Match and Write

3

The word *three* has a long **e** sound at the end.

SAY the name of the picture. FIND the correct name in the word box and CIRCLE it. Then WRITE the word.

| knee | bee | sheep | green | tree | queen |

_____
- - - - - - - - - - -
_____
1

_____
- - - - - - - - - - -
_____
2

_____
- - - - - - - - - - -
_____
3

_____
- - - - - - - - - - -
_____
4

_____
- - - - - - - - - - -
_____
5

_____
- - - - - - - - - - -
_____
6

What Am I?

WRITE the answers in the blanks. The words have the same vowel sound as the word *peel*.

I can make honey.

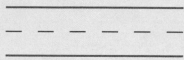

_ _ _ _ _

1

I am the color of trees and grass.

_ _ _ _ _

2

I can go around and around.

_ _ _ _ _

3

I come after two and before four.

_ _ _ _ _

4

I am part of a shoe.

_ _ _ _ _

5

Match Up

The word *mice* has a long **i** sound in the middle.

READ and TRACE each word. DRAW a line from the word to its matching picture.

 kite

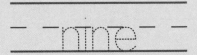 nine

 slide

 tie

 bike

Time to Rhyme

SAY the name of each picture. CIRCLE the word or words that rhyme.

1.    bite   cube   rope

2.    hive   save   keep

3. 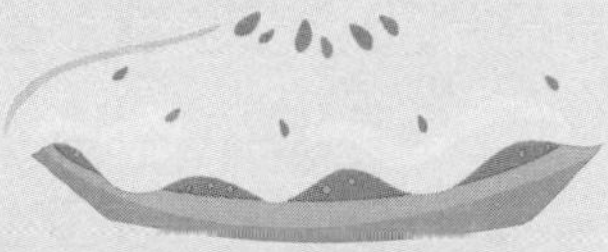   pole   pave   tie

4.    wipe   ripe   dive

5.    cone   fine   dine

6

Same Sound

The word *rose* has a long **o** in the middle.

SAY the name for each picture. WRITE "o" if you hear the long **o** sound.

Maze Crazy!

Help the goat get to the boat. DRAW a line through the maze to connect the pictures whose names have the long **o** sound.

6

Match and Write

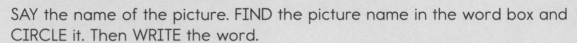

Hear the long **u** sound in the word *tune*.

SAY the name of the picture. FIND the picture name in the word box and CIRCLE it. Then WRITE the word.

| flute | blue | mule | glue | tube | cube |

1

2

3

4

5

6

Blank Out

READ each sentence and LOOK at the picture. WRITE the word to complete the sentence. LOOK at the word box for help.

mule	flute	blue	glue	cube

1. A _____ swam in the pool.

2. The spoon is by the _____.

3. The goose can play the _____.

4. The _____ is on the stool.

5. Luke has a _____ tuba.

7

It Takes Two

A COMPOUND word is made of two words. The two words are put together to make a new word.

WRITE the compound word made from each pair of pictures.

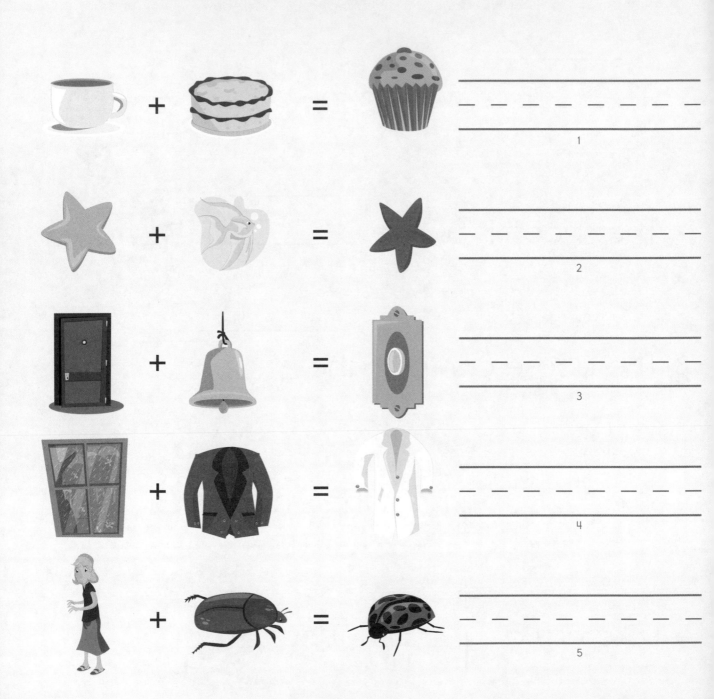

1 _____

2 _____

3 _____

4 _____

5 _____

One Plus One Makes Two

LOOK at the pictures. READ the words in the word box. WRITE the compound word that matches each pair of pictures.

football	doghouse	snowman	rainbow	catfish

\+ \=

‗ ‗ ‗ ‗ ‗ ‗ ‗ ‗ ‗ ‗
1

\+ \=

‗ ‗ ‗ ‗ ‗ ‗ ‗ ‗ ‗ ‗
2

\+ \=

‗ ‗ ‗ ‗ ‗ ‗ ‗ ‗ ‗ ‗
3

\+ \=

‗ ‗ ‗ ‗ ‗ ‗ ‗ ‗ ‗ ‗
4

\+ \=

‗ ‗ ‗ ‗ ‗ ‗ ‗ ‗ ‗ ‗
5

Double the Fun

When a word has two syllables with **double** consonants in the middle, such as *rabbit*, divide the word between the consonants: *rab | bit*.

DIVIDE the words into syllables. Then WRITE the syllables next to the words.

1. din|ner   din   ner

2. kitten   _____   _____

3. mitten   _____   _____

4. happen   _____   _____

5. puppet   _____   _____

6. zipper   _____   _____

7. muffin   _____   _____

8. button   _____   _____

Put It Together

LOOK at each picture and the syllable next to it. FILL IN the rest of each word with a syllable from the word box.

| low | za | ten | mer | ple | py |

1. ap _ple_

2. ham _____

3. mit _____

4. piz _____

5. pup _____

6. yel _____

8

Split It Up

When a word has two syllables with **any two consonants** in the middle, you can usually divide the word between the consonants.

DIVIDE the words into syllables. Then WRITE the syllables next to the words.

1. nap|kin   nap   kin

2. basket

3. doctor

4. picnic

5. monkey

6. winter

7. sister

8. pencil

Put It Together

SAY the name for each animal. FILL IN the rest of each word with a syllable from the word box.

pen	wal	mon	ur	tur	roos

1.  _____ rus

2.  _____ key

3.  _____ tle

4.  _____ ter

5.  _____ key

6.  _____ guin

9

Stack Up

LOOK at the words and pictures. WRITE the names of the pictures in the correct columns.

lemon

corn

apple

carrot

orange

grapes

broccoli

lettuce

Fruits

_____

- - - - - - - - - - - - -

_____

- - - - - - - - - - - - -

_____

- - - - - - - - - - - - -

_____

- - - - - - - - - - - - -

_____

Vegetables

_____

- - - - - - - - - - - - -

_____

- - - - - - - - - - - - -

_____

- - - - - - - - - - - - -

_____

- - - - - - - - - - - - -

_____

Odd Word Out

CIRCLE the picture in each row that does **not** go with the others.

1.

cookies   cupcake   olive   pie

2.

ladybug   butterfly   dog   bee

3.

yarn   pants   dress   shirt

WRITE the names of the pictures that do **not** belong.

_____   _____
- - - - - - - - - - - -   - - - - - - - - - - - -
_____   _____
             1   2

_____
- - - - - - - - - - - -
_____
             3

9

Stack Up

LOOK at the words and pictures. WRITE the names of the pictures in the correct columns.

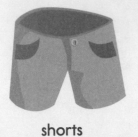

shorts

sandals

earmuffs

swimsuit

scarf

mittens

Summer Clothes

_____

- - - - - - - - - - -

_____

- - - - - - - - - - -

_____

- - - - - - - - - - -

_____

Winter Clothes

_____

- - - - - - - - - - -

_____

- - - - - - - - - - -

_____

- - - - - - - - - - -

_____

Odd Word Out

CIRCLE the picture in each row that does **not** go with the others.

1.

five   green   yellow   blue

2.

goat   cow   zebra   pig

3.

bat   rake   hoe   shovel

WRITE the names of the pictures that do **not** belong.

_____   _____
- - - - - - - - - - - -   - - - - - - - - - - - -
_____   _____
          1   2
_____
- - - - - - - - - - - -
_____
          3

It's All in the Picture

The **main idea** is the most important idea in a story. It's the big idea. It tells what the story is about.

READ the story and CIRCLE the picture that best tells the story's main idea.

Best Friends

Marta and Nicky are best friends. They walk to school together. They ride bikes together. They read books together. They play ball together. Marta and Nicky do everything together.

Name It

READ the story. CHECK the box next to the best title for the story.

Rosa is a baker. One of the best cakes she ever made was for a man named Mr. Lee. He wanted a special cake for his wife's birthday party. Mrs. Lee loves cats. So Rosa made her a cake with cats on it.

Mrs. Lee thought the cake was the best cake she had ever seen. She did not want to cut it. Mr. Lee said that their guests were waiting to eat cake. Mrs. Lee almost cried when she had to cut the cake. But she loved the way it tasted.

☐ A Special Cake

☐ Cats Are Special

☐ A Birthday Party

First, Next, Last

A story has a beginning, a middle, and an end. READ the story. What happens first? Next? Last? WRITE 1, 2, and 3 in the boxes to show the correct order.

Time to Garden

"Time to get up!" said Mom and Dad.

"Why?" asked Kate and Tim.

"We're going to plant a garden," said Mom and Dad.

Kate and Tim got up and got dressed. Then they ate breakfast.

Mom, Dad, Kate, and Tim drove to the garden shop. They bought flower seeds and some gardening tools.

When they got home, Dad dug up the dirt. Kate and Tim poked holes in the dirt. Kate and Tim put a few seeds in each hole. Then they covered the holes with dirt. Mom watered the seeds.

"Now we just have to wait," said Dad. "The plants will grow into pretty flowers," said Mom.

Kate and Tim smiled.

☐ Mom waters the garden.

☐ Kate and Tim plant the seeds.

☐ Dad digs up the dirt.

READ the story. What happens first? Next? Last? WRITE 1, 2, and 3 in the boxes to show the correct order.

Market Day

Today is market day. First Grandma and Juan stop by to see Mr. Sanchez the baker. The air is filled with delicious smells. Grandma buys two loaves of bread. When they leave, Mr. Sanchez hands Juan a cookie.

Their next stop is the fruit stand. They buy grapes, peaches, and plums. Grandma gets some flowers just before they leave.

At home, Grandma puts the flowers in a vase and Juan unpacks the food. Then he eats a ripe, juicy peach.

☐ Grandma and Juan stop at the baker's.

☐ Juan eats a peach.

☐ Grandma buys some flowers.

Picture Order

Sometimes stories have words like "first," "next," "after," and "last." These words give you clues about the order of events in the story.

LOOK at the pictures and READ the sentences. LOOK for the word clues. Then NUMBER the pictures from 1 to 4 to show the order in the stories.

Then Alex looks under the bed. She is not behind the door. She is not under the bed.

After Mom hides, Alex looks behind the door. She is not there.

Alex looks in the closet last. There is Mom!

Mom hides first.

Finally, Mia puts the leaves into a big bag.

Then Mia rakes the leaves into a big pile.

First, Mia gets a rake.

Next, Mia begins to rake.

12 Making Predictions

Pick the One

Sometimes you can tell or *predict* what a book is about by looking at the picture on the cover.

LOOK at the picture on each cover. CIRCLE the title that best shows what the story might be about.

1.
   a. *Time to Garden*
   b. *Learn to Skate*
   c. *Leaves Are Changing*

2.
   a. *Many Animals Live in Ponds*
   b. *Ducks and Other Birds*
   c. *Frog and Turtle Are Friends*

3.
   a. *Water Play*
   b. *Dog Wash*
   c. *Time to Swim*

Detective Work

READ the story and LOOK for clues. PREDICT what will happen next. WRITE your prediction on the blank line.

Rosie's Problem

Rosie shook the coins out of her piggy bank. She had been saving for a long time. She counted the coins. She had saved ten dollars. But Rosie had a big problem. She did not know what to buy with her money. She asked her mom. She asked her dad. She even asked her little brother. No one had an answer. Mom said, "Why don't we go to the toy store?"

There were so many toys. Rosie looked at the toy cars. She looked at the dolls. She looked at the games. Rosie was sad. She did not know how to spend her money. "Let's just go home, Mom," Rosie sighed.

Someone was holding a box of puppies in front of the toy store. Rosie stopped and read the sign on the box. A big smile spread across her face. She knew exactly what to do.

How do you think Rosie most likely spent her money?

Rosie most likely spent her money on

_____

_ _

Making Predictions

12

And Then . . .

READ the beginning of the story. Then PREDICT what will happen next.
UNDERLINE the correct answer.

Sam's Vacation

Sam is going to stay with his uncle and aunt for the summer. They live on a farm.

Sam's mother grew up on a farm. She told Sam stories about how much fun she had on the farm. Sam was excited. But he worried about being away from home all summer. "There is so much to do," said Sam's mother. "You'll love it."

Sam was surprised when he first saw the farm. It looked so different from where he lived. He was used to seeing many cars and big buildings. Here he saw only a white house and a red barn.

The next morning, Sam woke up early. His uncle showed him how to milk a cow. After lunch, he learned how to feed the chickens and pigs.

After dinner, Sam got a phone call. It was his mother. She asked, "Did you enjoy your day?"

"I sure did," Sam said excitedly. "I can't wait for tomorrow."

What do you think Sam will do tomorrow?

a. Milk the cow and feed the chickens and pigs

b. Ask to go home

c. Stay inside all day

Section 2:
Summer Smart Math

Counting & Numbering to 10

Connect the Dots

DRAW a line to connect the numbers in order, starting with 1.

Criss Cross

WRITE each number word with one letter in each square.

Across ➔   Down ↓

3.   1.

4.   2.

5.   3.

7.   6.

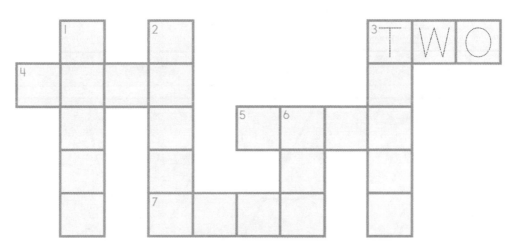

Mystery Number

WRITE the sums, and COLOR each section according to the numbers to reveal the mystery number. 8 = 10 = 5 = 4 = 7 =

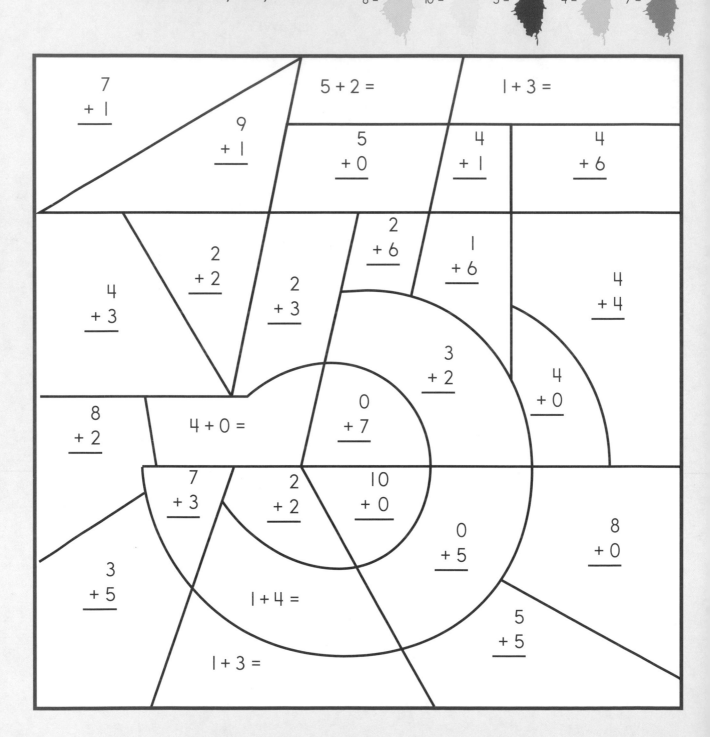

Safe Crackers

WRITE the sums. Then WRITE the sums from smallest to largest to find the right combination for the safe.

$$\begin{array}{r} 5 \\ +2 \\ \hline \end{array}$$ 7

$$\begin{array}{r} 3 \\ +3 \\ \hline \end{array}$$

$$\begin{array}{r} 1 \\ +4 \\ \hline \end{array}$$

$$\begin{array}{r} 1 \\ +1 \\ \hline \end{array}$$

$$\begin{array}{r} 6 \\ +3 \\ \hline \end{array}$$

$$\begin{array}{r} 8 \\ +0 \\ \hline \end{array}$$

1   2   3   4   5   6

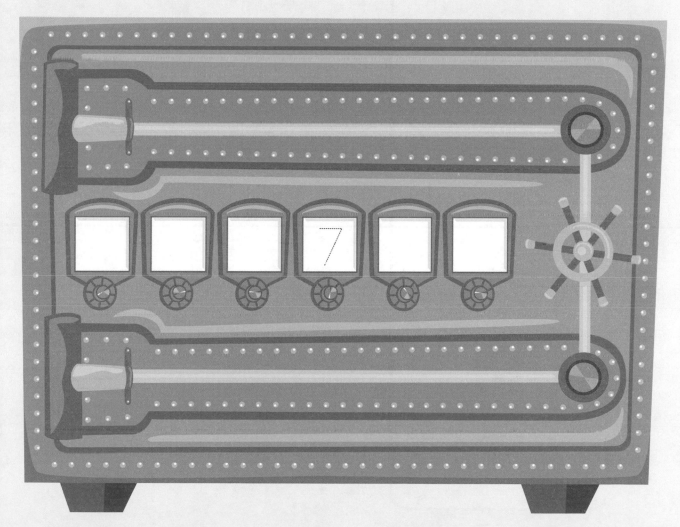

Your Deal

Using the number cards 2 through 7 from a deck of playing cards, DEAL a card onto each space. SAY the sum out loud. REPEAT until you have run out of cards.

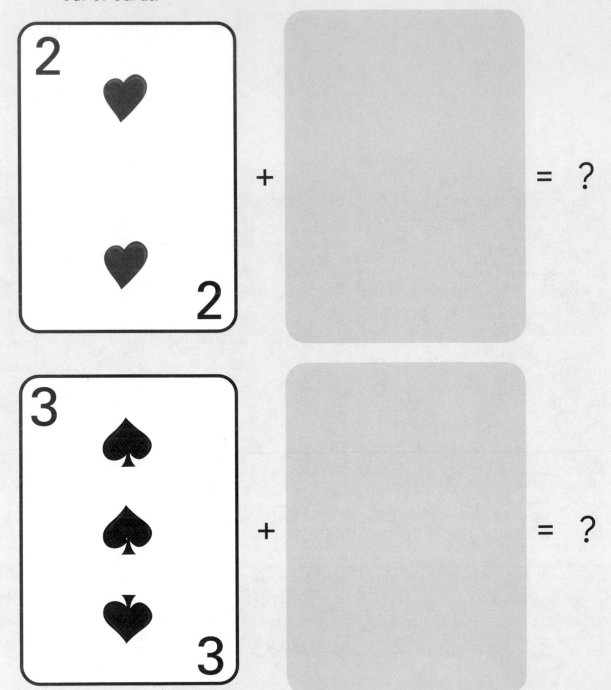

Code Breaker

SOLVE each problem. Then WRITE the letter or number that matches each sum to solve the riddle.

3	8	5	2	3	1
+ 1	+ 2	+ 4	+ 4	+ 5	+ 0
4					
1	2	3	4	5	6
U	B	A	7	S	8

4	5	2
+ 1	+ 2	+ 1
7	8	9
E	9	C

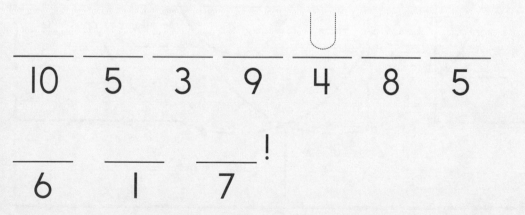

Why is 6 afraid of 7?

____ ____ ____ ____ U____ ____ ____
10   5   3   9   4   8   5

____ ____ ____!
6   1   7

Subtracting Differences from 10

Mystery Number

WRITE the differences, and COLOR each section according to the differences to reveal the mystery number.

1 = 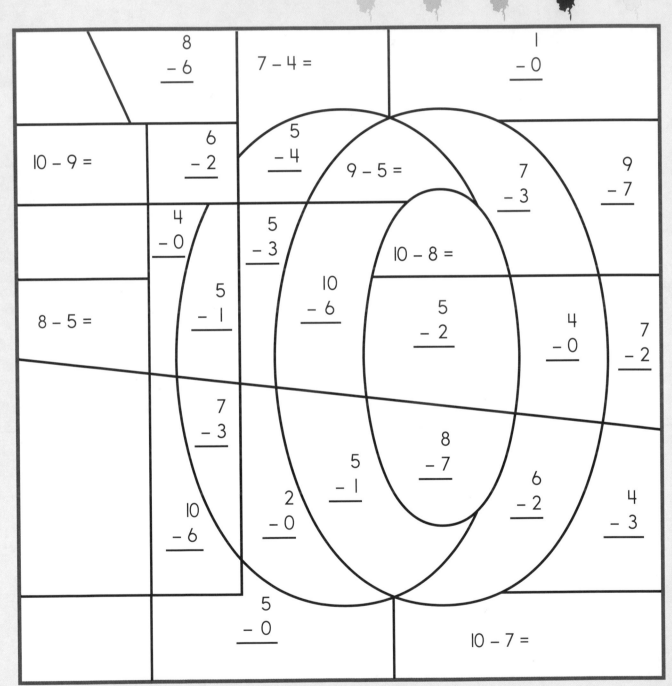 2 =   3 =   4 =   5 =

$$\begin{array}{r} 8 \\ -6 \\ \hline \end{array}$$

$$7 - 4 =$$

$$\begin{array}{r} 1 \\ -0 \\ \hline \end{array}$$

$$10 - 9 =$$

$$\begin{array}{r} 6 \\ -2 \\ \hline \end{array}$$

$$\begin{array}{r} 5 \\ -4 \\ \hline \end{array}$$

$$9 - 5 =$$

$$\begin{array}{r} 7 \\ -3 \\ \hline \end{array}$$

$$\begin{array}{r} 9 \\ -7 \\ \hline \end{array}$$

$$\begin{array}{r} 4 \\ -0 \\ \hline \end{array}$$

$$\begin{array}{r} 5 \\ -3 \\ \hline \end{array}$$

$$10 - 8 =$$

$$8 - 5 =$$

$$\begin{array}{r} 5 \\ -1 \\ \hline \end{array}$$

$$\begin{array}{r} 10 \\ -6 \\ \hline \end{array}$$

$$\begin{array}{r} 5 \\ -2 \\ \hline \end{array}$$

$$\begin{array}{r} 4 \\ -0 \\ \hline \end{array}$$

$$\begin{array}{r} 7 \\ -2 \\ \hline \end{array}$$

$$\begin{array}{r} 7 \\ -3 \\ \hline \end{array}$$

$$\begin{array}{r} 8 \\ -7 \\ \hline \end{array}$$

$$\begin{array}{r} 10 \\ -6 \\ \hline \end{array}$$

$$\begin{array}{r} 2 \\ -0 \\ \hline \end{array}$$

$$\begin{array}{r} 5 \\ -1 \\ \hline \end{array}$$

$$\begin{array}{r} 6 \\ -2 \\ \hline \end{array}$$

$$\begin{array}{r} 4 \\ -3 \\ \hline \end{array}$$

$$\begin{array}{r} 5 \\ -0 \\ \hline \end{array}$$

$$10 - 7 =$$

Safe Crackers

WRITE the differences. Then WRITE the differences from largest to smallest to find the right combination for the safe.

$$\begin{array}{r} 10 \\ -\ 8 \\ \hline \end{array}$$
1

$$\begin{array}{r} 5 \\ -\ 1 \\ \hline \end{array}$$
2

$$\begin{array}{r} 6 \\ -\ 3 \\ \hline \end{array}$$
3

$$\begin{array}{r} 9 \\ -\ 1 \\ \hline \end{array}$$
4

$$\begin{array}{r} 8 \\ -\ 2 \\ \hline \end{array}$$
5

$$\begin{array}{r} 7 \\ -\ 7 \\ \hline \end{array}$$
6

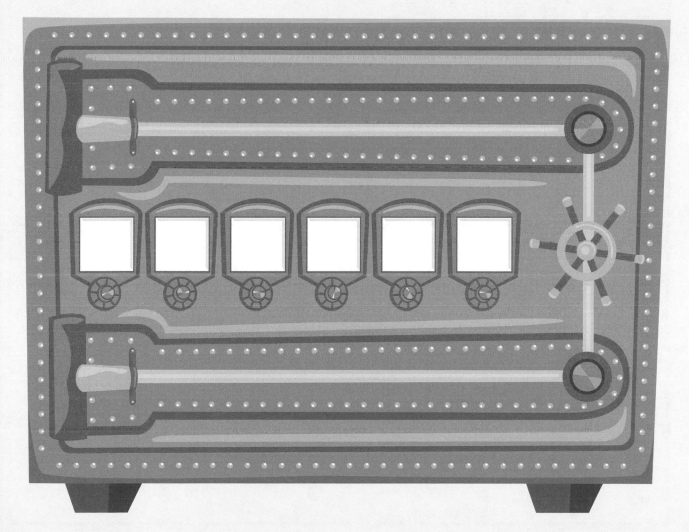

Pipe Down

WRITE the missing number. Then FOLLOW the pipe, and WRITE the same number in the next problem.

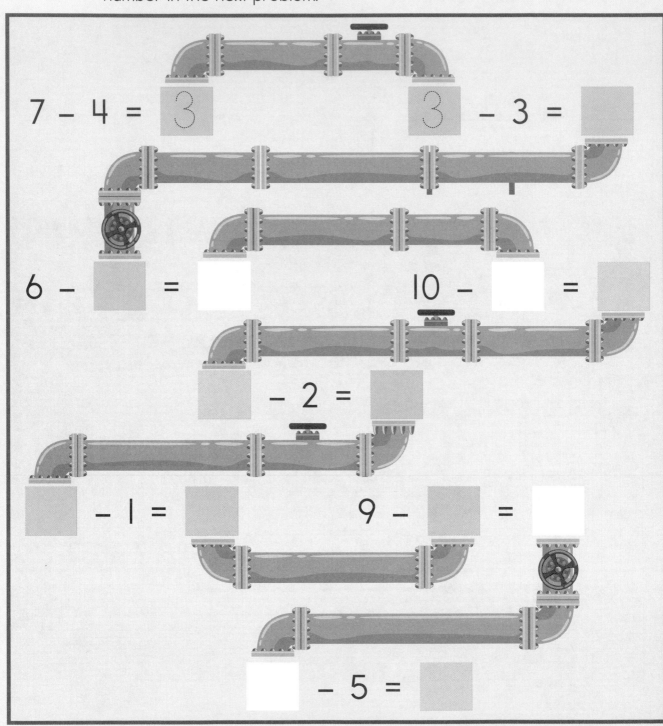

7 – 4 = 3

3 – 3 =

6 – ☐ = ☐

10 – ☐ =

☐ – 2 =

☐ – 1 = ☐

9 – ☐ = ☐

☐ – 5 = ☐

Space Walk

Using the numbers in the picture, WRITE as many fact families with the number 9 as you can.

HINT: A fact family shows all of the different ways that three numbers can be added and subtracted.

Example: 1 + 2 = 3
2 + 1 = 3
3 − 1 = 2
3 − 2 = 1

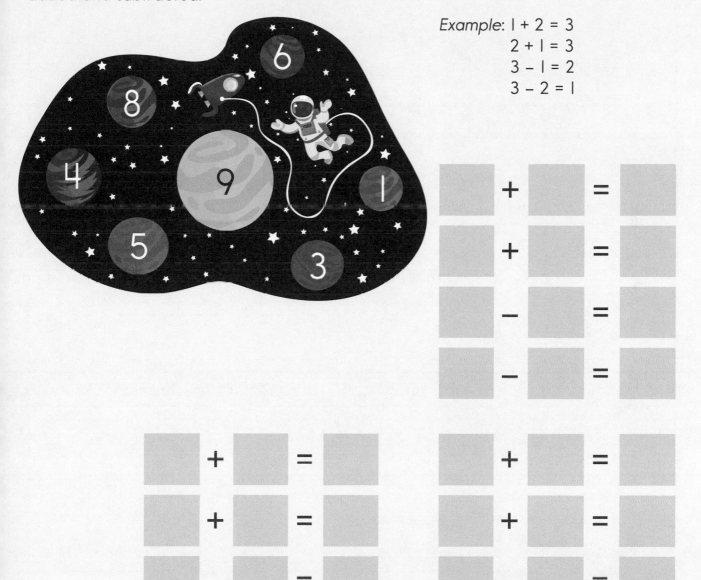

Connect the Dots

DRAW a line to connect the numbers in order, starting with 1.

Criss Cross

WRITE each number word with one letter in each square.

Across ➡

2. 15

3. 13

4. 12

5. 19

Down ↓

1. 20

2. 14

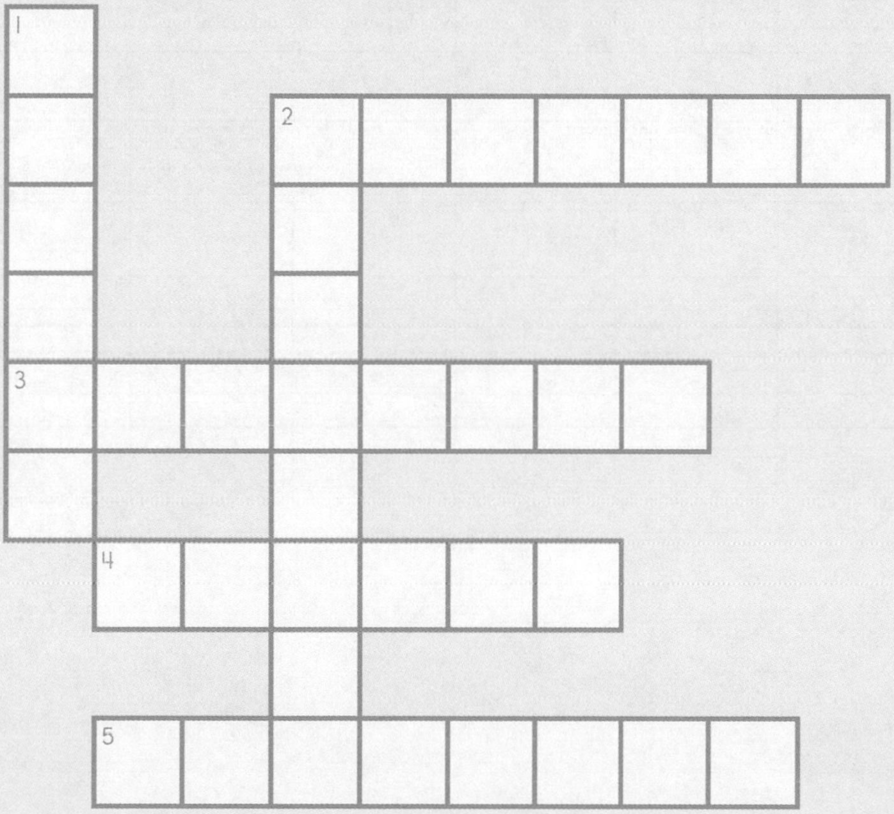

Counting & Numbering to 20

Hidden Design

COUNT the dots. Then COLOR the squares to see the hidden design.

16	16	16	16	16	16	16	13
19	19	19	19	19	19	13	16
17	17	17	17	17	13	19	16
12	12	12	12	13	17	19	16
14	14	14	13	12	17	19	16
18	18	13	14	12	17	19	16
11	13	18	14	12	17	19	16
13	11	18	14	12	17	19	16

Ant Farm

The signs are in the wrong places. DRAW a line from each sign to the ant farm where it belongs.

15 Ants

16 Ants

18 Ants

14 Ants

Safe Crackers

WRITE the sums. Then WRITE the sums from smallest to largest to find the right combination for the safe.

$$\begin{array}{r} 7 \\ + 8 \\ \hline \end{array}$$

$$\begin{array}{r} 10 \\ + 10 \\ \hline \end{array}$$

$$\begin{array}{r} 3 \\ + 9 \\ \hline \end{array}$$

$$\begin{array}{r} 6 \\ + 5 \\ \hline \end{array}$$

$$\begin{array}{r} 9 \\ + 9 \\ \hline \end{array}$$

$$\begin{array}{r} 8 \\ + 6 \\ \hline \end{array}$$

1   2   3   4   5   6

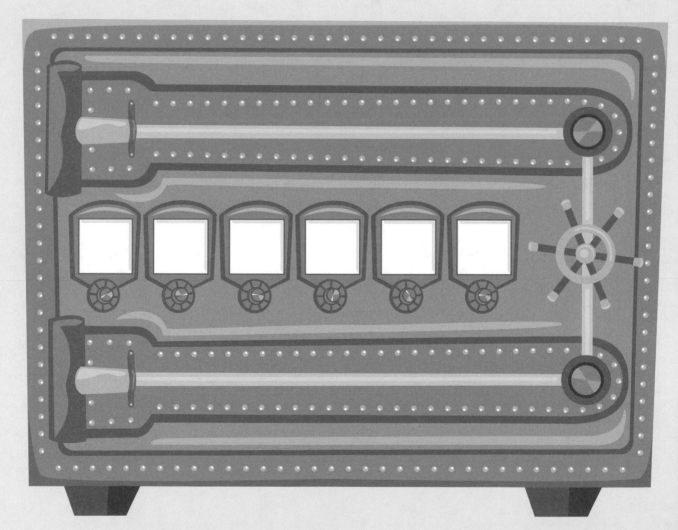

Code Breaker

SOLVE each problem. Then WRITE the letter that matches each sum to solve the riddle.

9 + 4	11 + 8	5 + 6	8 + 7	14 + 4	10 +10
1	2	3	4	5	6
H	V	I	A	M	O

12 + 2	6 + 6	7 + 9
7	8	9
T	E	S

Where did the cow spend her afternoon?

___ ___ ___ ___ ___
15 14   14 13 12

___ ___ ___ ___ ___ ___ ___!
18 20 20 19 11 12 16

Your Deal

Using the number cards 2 through 10 from a deck of playing cards, DEAL a card onto each space. SAY the sum out loud. REPEAT until you have run out of cards.

 + = ?

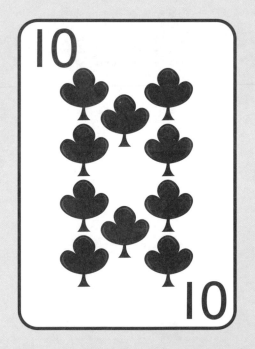 + = ?

5

Crossing Paths

WRITE the missing numbers.

Left puzzle:

1		2
+		+
	2	
=		=
○		○
+		+
	3	
=		=
○		○
+		+
	4	
=		=
○		○
+		+
	6	
=		=
○		○
+		+
	1	
=		=
○		○

Right puzzle:

2		3
+		+
	0	
=		=
○		○
+		+
	6	
=		=
○		○
+		+
	5	
=		=
○		○
+		+
	1	
=		=
○		○
+		+
	5	
=		=
○		○

Subtracting Differences from 20

Missing Middles

WRITE the number missing from the center square.

1.

```
      15
      —
11 —  [ ] = 3
      =
      7
```

2.

```
      12
      —
20 —  [ ] = 9
      =
      1
```

3.

```
      17
      —
16 —  [ ] = 14
      =
      15
```

4.

```
      18
      —
13 —  [ ] = 4
      =
      9
```

5.

```
      20
      —
19 —  [ ] = 4
      =
      5
```

6.

```
      14
      —
18 —  [ ] = 15
      =
      11
```

Safe Crackers

WRITE the differences. Then WRITE the differences from largest to smallest to find the right combination for the safe.

19 − 7	14 − 8	11 − 2	20 − 2	16 −11	13 −12
1	2	3	4	5	6

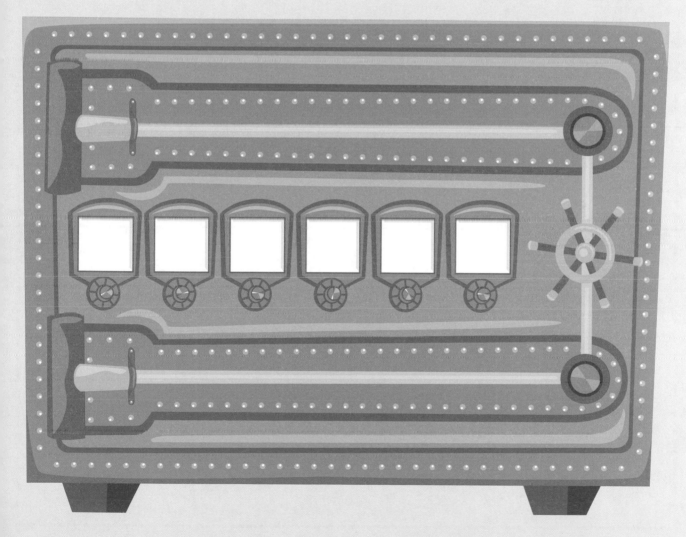

Subtracting Differences from 20

Pipe Down

WRITE the missing number. Then FOLLOW the pipe, and WRITE the same number in the next problem.

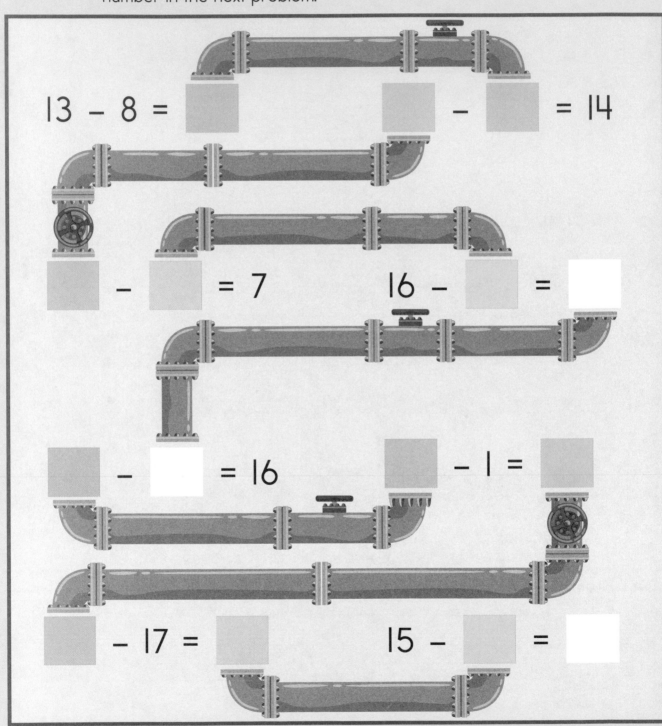

13 – 8 = ☐   ☐ – ☐ = 14

☐ – ☐ = 7   16 – ☐ = ☐

☐ – ☐ = 16   ☐ – 1 = ☐

☐ – 17 = ☐   15 – ☐ = ☐

Space Walk

Using the numbers in the picture, WRITE as many
fact families with the number 17 as you can.

☐ + ☐ = ☐

☐ + ☐ = ☐

☐ − ☐ = ☐

☐ − ☐ = ☐

☐ + ☐ = ☐   ☐ + ☐ = ☐

☐ + ☐ = ☐   ☐ + ☐ = ☐

☐ − ☐ = ☐   ☐ − ☐ = ☐

☐ − ☐ = ☐   ☐ − ☐ = ☐

Color Mix-up

These squares are all the right colors, but they're in the wrong order. COLOR the squares on the opposite page the same color as the numbers on this page to see the design.

45	52	8	81	17	93	37	14	61	28
18	23	79	58	72	30	78	51	13	80
60	71	67	22	89	48	35	86	68	94
9	46	96	26	1	34	65	41	100	16
88	74	19	85	95	73	57	87	29	77
27	4	66	49	36	15	99	2	47	59
33	11	92	12	31	43	84	64	25	7
76	53	3	62	50	5	55	21	56	97
42	38	82	70	63	90	75	44	91	40
10	98	32	54	20	24	83	39	6	69

1	2	3	4	5	6	7	8	9	10
11	12	13	14	15	16	17	18	19	20
21	22	23	24	25	26	27	28	29	30
31	32	33	34	35	36	37	38	39	40
41	42	43	44	45	46	47	48	49	50
51	52	53	54	55	56	57	58	59	60
61	62	63	64	65	66	67	68	69	70
71	72	73	74	75	76	77	78	79	80
81	82	83	84	85	86	87	88	89	90
91	92	93	94	95	96	97	98	99	100

Super Spies

WRITE the missing numbers in the chart. DECODE the note on the opposite page, using the letters in those squares.

1	^O 2	3	4	5	6	7	8	^C	10
11	12	^L	^T	15	16	17	^N	19	20
21	22	23	24	25	26	27	28	29	30
31	32	33	34	35	^P	37	38	39	^E
41	^S	43	44	45	46	47	48	49	50
51	52	53	^V	55	56	57	58	^I	60
^K	62	63	64	65	66	^H	68	69	70
71	72	73	74	75	76	77	78	79	80
81	82	83	84	^A	86	87	88	89	90
^R	92	93	94	95	96	97	98	99	^D

‾‾‾ ‾‾‾ ‾‾‾   ‾‾‾ ‾‾‾ ‾‾‾ ‾‾‾ ‾‾‾ ‾‾‾
14   67   40   42   40   9   91   40   14

‾‾‾ ‾‾‾ ‾‾‾ ‾‾‾ ‾‾‾   ‾‾‾ ‾‾‾ ‾‾‾
36   13   85   18   42   85   91   40

‾‾‾ ‾‾‾ ‾‾‾ ‾‾‾ ‾‾‾ ‾‾‾   ‾‾‾ ‾‾‾
67   59   100   100   40   18   59   18

‾‾‾ ‾‾‾ ‾‾‾   ‾‾‾ ‾‾‾ ‾‾‾ ‾‾‾
14   67   40   54   85   42   40

◯
‾‾‾ ‾‾‾   ‾‾‾ ‾‾‾ ‾‾‾
2   18   14   67   40

‾‾‾ ‾‾‾ ‾‾‾ ‾‾‾ .
100   40   42   61

Hidden Design

COUNT the tens and ones. Then COLOR the squares that match the numbers to see the hidden design.

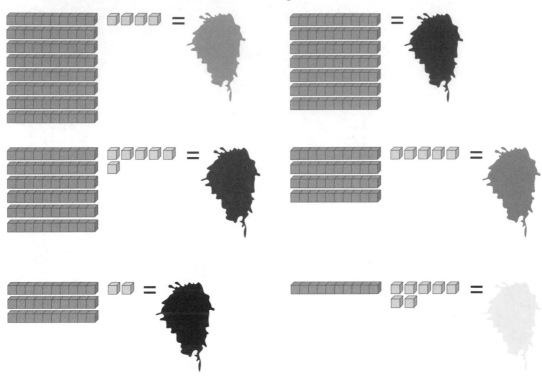

66	66	66	66	66	66	66	66
66	84	84	84	84	84	84	84
84	84	17	17	17	17	17	17
17	17	17	45	45	45	45	45
45	45	45	45	32	32	32	32
32	32	32	32	32	70	70	70
70	70	70	70	70	70	66	66
66	66	66	66	66	66	66	84

Safe Crackers

WRITE the number for each picture. Then WRITE the digit in the tens place of each number from largest to smallest to find the combination for the safe.

43		
1	2	3
4	5	6

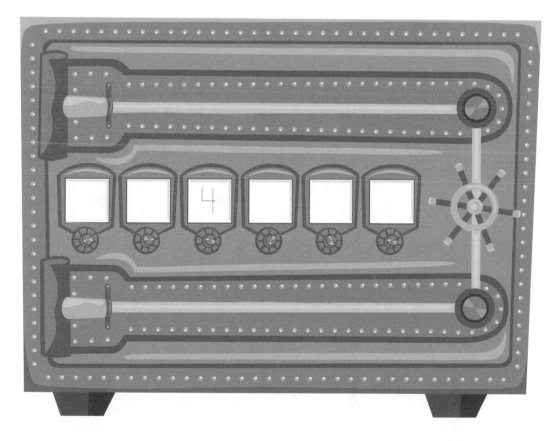

Number Search

WRITE the number for each picture. Then CIRCLE it in the puzzle.
HINT: Numbers are across and down only.

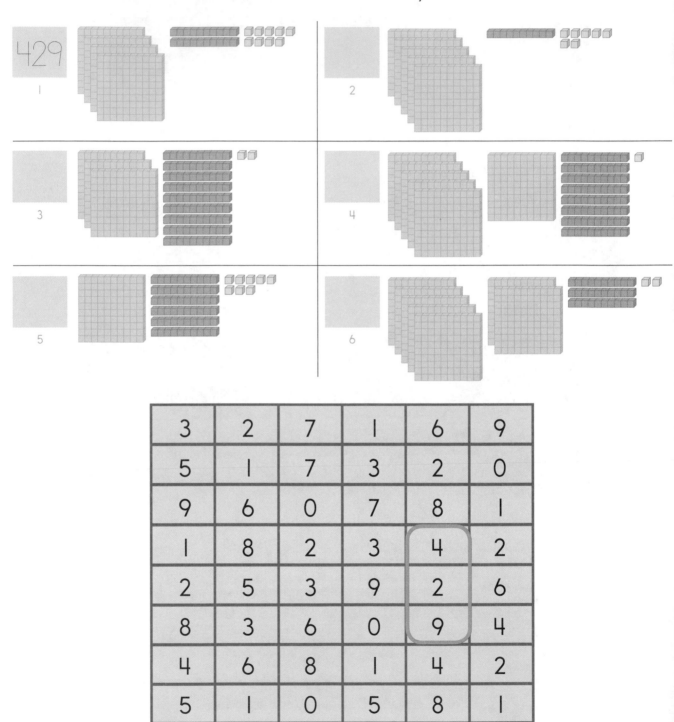

Code Breaker

WRITE the number for each picture. Then WRITE the letter that matches each number to solve the riddle.

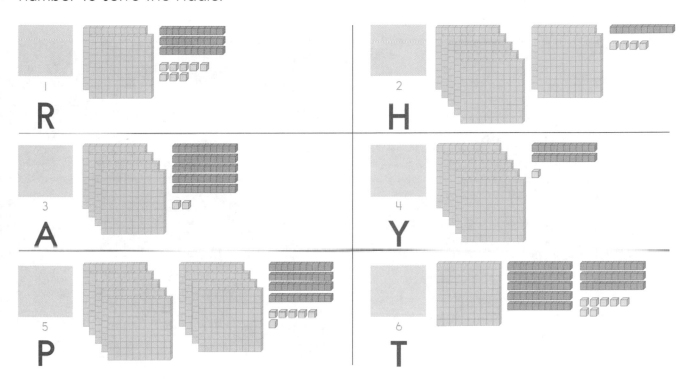

1. **R**

2. **H**

3. **A**

4. **Y**

5. **P**

6. **T**

What did the pirate wear to his birthday party?

$$\overline{}$$
452

$$\overline{}\ \overline{}\ \overline{}\ \overline{}\ \overline{}\ \overline{}\ \overline{}$$
946 452 238 238 238 187 521

$$\overline{}\ \overline{}\ \overline{}\ .$$
714 452 187

Number Lines & Patterns

Where's My Brain?

START at the arrow. DRAW a path by skip counting by 2 to reach the brain. HINT: Skip counting is like adding 2 to each number. For example: 1, 3, 5, 7, and so on.

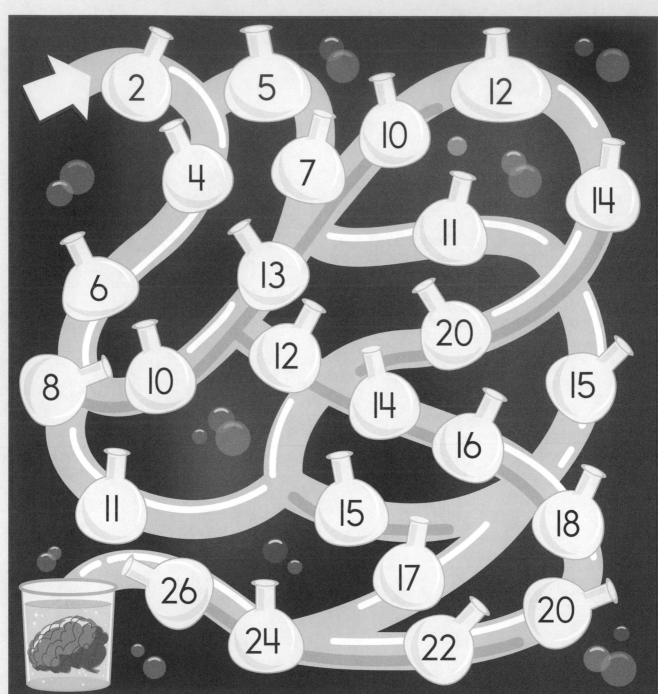

Roll It

ROLL a number cube, and WRITE the number in the first box. ROLL it again and write the number in the second box. Then WRITE the next six numbers, skip counting by the difference between the first two numbers.

Example:

+3   +3

| 2 | 5 | 8 | 11 | 14 | 17 | 20 | 23 |

Comparing Numbers

Find the Fountain

START at the arrow, and DRAW the correct path to the center fountain. When there is a choice of numbers, follow the smaller number.

Win Big

Wherever two boxes point to one box, WRITE the larger number. START at the sides and work toward the center to see which number will win big.

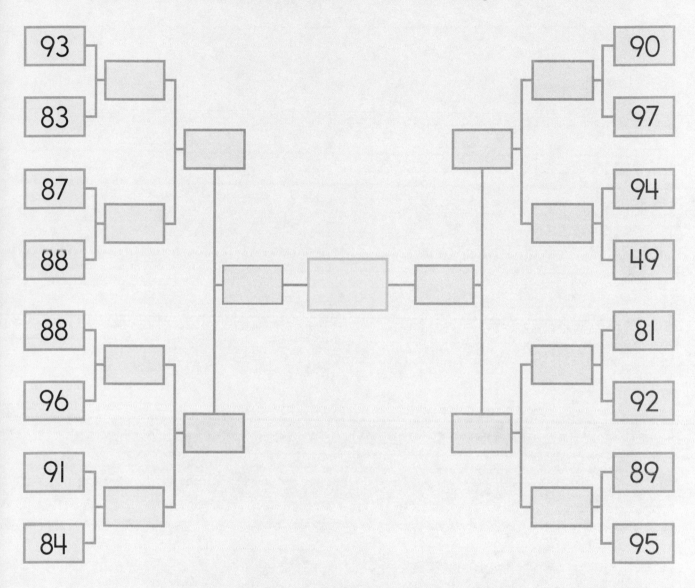

Drawing & Comparing Shapes

Picture Perfect

DRAW different size rectangles to make buildings. Then DRAW doors and windows and COLOR the buildings.

Hidden Shapes

FIND each shape hidden in the picture. DRAW a line to connect each shape with its location in the picture.

Doodle Pad

TRACE the shapes. Then DRAW a picture using each shape.

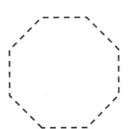

Sneaky Shapes

WRITE the number of triangles and rectangles you see.

HINT: Think about the different ways smaller shapes can make larger shapes, like when four small triangles make a larger triangle.

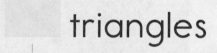 triangles

rectangles

13

Incredible Illusions

COLOR the picture so it is symmetrical. When you're done coloring, LOOK at the picture. Do you see two faces or a candlestick?

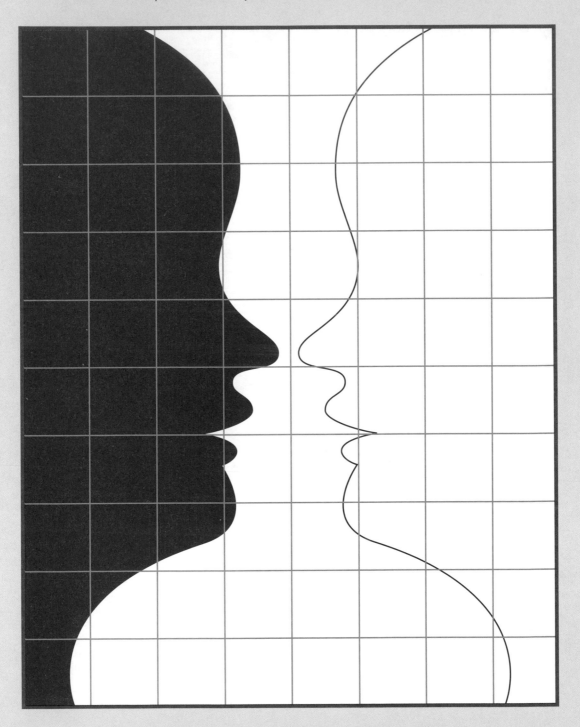

Cool Kaleidoscope

COLOR the kaleidoscope so it is symmetrical.

HINT: Work across the top, then make
the bottom a mirror image of the top.

14

House Hunt

HUNT around your home to FIND eight things longer than this line of 5 paper clips. WRITE what you find.

Picking Pairs

LINE UP pennies and MEASURE each wand. DRAW a line connecting pairs of wands that are the same length.

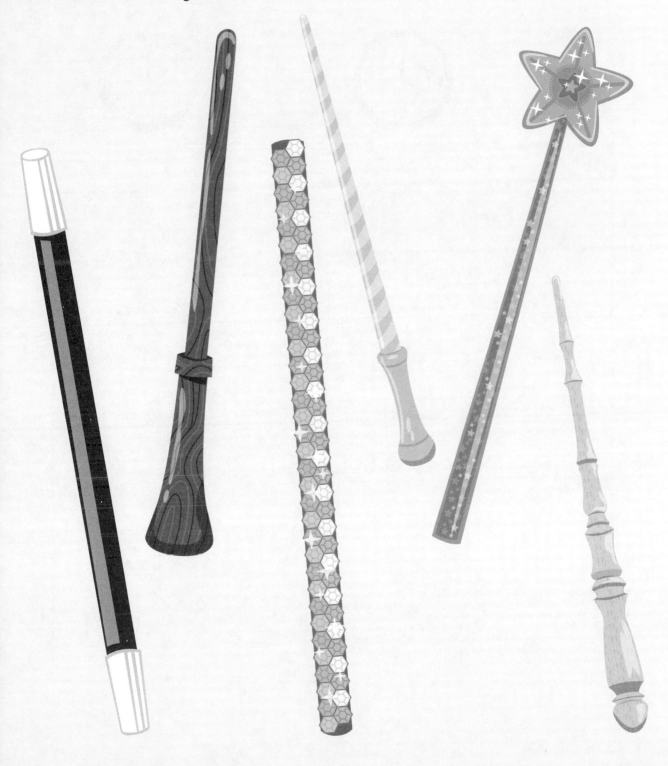

Mystery Time

COLOR the times in the picture according to the color of the clocks at the top. When you are done coloring, WRITE the mystery time under the picture.

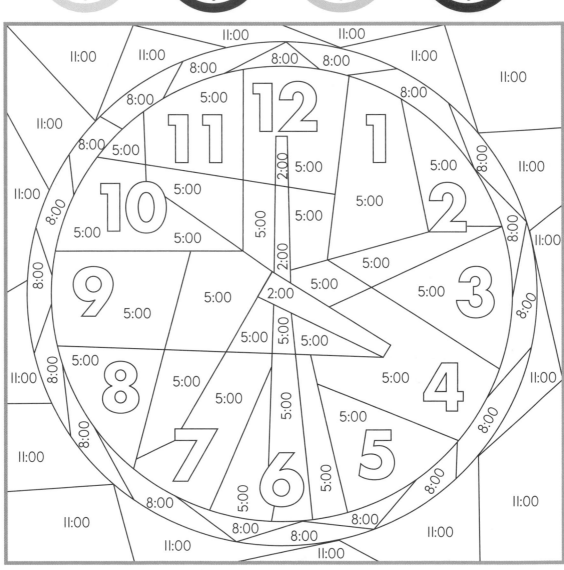

:00

Time Travel

DRAW a line from Start through the clocks to get to the end, traveling ahead one hour as you go from clock to clock.

Start

End

What's My Time?

READ the clues, and CIRCLE the clock with the correct time.

I'm next to at least one clock that is later than I am.

I'm not usually a time when you would eat a meal.

If I'm at night, you're probably asleep.

I'm a half hour later than one of my neighbors.

Pocket Change

DRAW exactly two lines to create four different sets of coins of equal value.

Code Breaker

WRITE the value of each coin or coin set. Then WRITE the letter that matches each value to solve the riddle.

1	2	3	4	5
S	**W**	**K**	**B**	**I**

6	7	8
N	**A**	**O**

Where does the penguin keep his money?

___ ___ ___   ___ ___ ___ ___
20¢ 15¢ 36¢   1¢ 15¢ 17¢ 25¢

___ ___ ___ ___!
11¢ 36¢ 15¢ 5¢

Money Maze

DRAW a line to get from the start of the maze to the end, crossing exactly enough coins to total the end amount.

HINT: There's more than one way through the maze, but you must follow the path that totals 82¢.

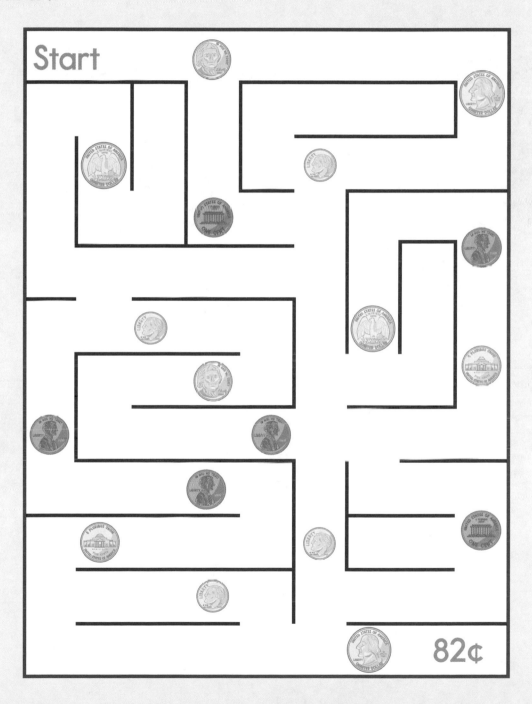

Using Coins

Slide Sort

CIRCLE the coins that are **not** enough money to pay for the object at the bottom of the slide.

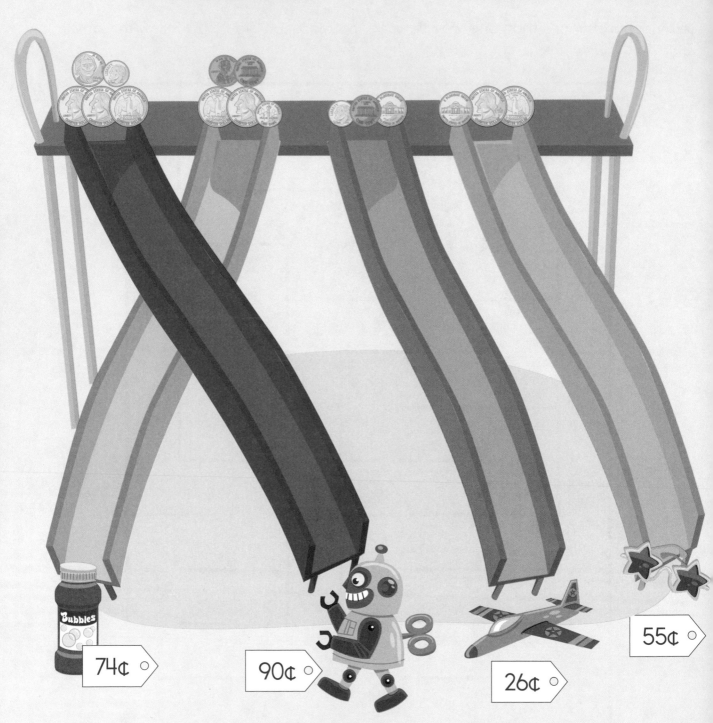

Section 3:
Vacation Challenge
Games & Activities

Vacation Challenge Contents

Tips for Summer Reading Success

Try these terrific read-aloud tips to jumpstart your child's summer reading!

Let your child see YOU reading. Children imitate what we do as adults, so seeing you deep in a book will help your child view reading as a fun and valuable activity.

Get into the habit of going to the library. Head to the library together often—even if your home is overflowing with books! Making the library an exciting destination will help your child see that people of all ages are readers and that reading is a way of life, not just a classroom activity.

Rereading is magical. Encourage your child to reread favorite books and poems. Rereading develops accuracy and builds confidence.

Be patient! Allow time for your child to sound out unfamiliar words. As your child tries to tackle new words, remind her to use clues such as the first letter of the word, the vowel sound, or the context.

Take turns as an easy way to increase interactivity. Kids love taking turns reading with their parents, especially at bedtime. Switch between the two of you while reading sentences, pages, or chapters, depending on your child's reading level.

The end of the story is only the beginning! Ask your child questions about the characters, the setting, and the story's problem and solution. Most importantly, ask "why" questions that will help your child think. (We've included some suggestions later in this section to help you get started.)

Reading and writing go hand-in-hand. Write notes to your child! Children love a surprise note on their dresser or in their lunchbox. This will give your child an understanding of the value of reading for authentic communication purposes. She can also practice her own writing—for example, invite her to help you with your grocery list before heading to the supermarket. List-writing is a perfect first grade skill because it is short and sweet, and it promotes success.

Wonderful Word Activities

Embark on an awesome adventure this summer with these fun activities that will help your child practice writing, vocabulary, and early reading skills!

Alphabet Scattergories.

This writing exercise is both creative and fun! Write the alphabet vertically down the left side of a piece of paper. Choose a category (such as "Fruits and Vegetables" or "Animals") and write it at the top. Now, beside each letter, write a word that starts with that letter and fits into the category. It can be quite a challenge to complete the entire alphabet, but you can always work together as a family or look in a dictionary for clues.

Edible Words.

Using alphabet crackers, cookies, or cereal pieces, have your child spell and read sight words...and then EAT them! A more advanced variation is to have your child create words and/or sentences from the alphabet pieces.

Syllable Snaps.

Have fun with syllables by snapping your fingers or clapping your hands to the beats (syllables) in your name. Try this for all of the members of your family and keep track of how many syllables each name has. Then let the fun continue by snapping/clapping the syllables in the names of cartoon characters, sports figures, animals, and anything else that catches your child's attention!

Reading Scavenger Hunt.

Design a simple reading scavenger hunt for your child using written clues and books from around your house. Write the clues on a piece of paper and give the paper to your child. Now, he has to read the clues and find the books that match each clue in order to complete the hunt. (Example clues: find a book with the word "brown" in the title; find a book with 5 chapters; find a book about a president; find a book written by Dr. Seuss; etc.)

Sticker Sentences.

Let your child choose three to five stickers to use in writing a rebus sentence. Help her plan her sentence ahead of time on scrap paper. Then have her print the sentence on a piece of paper, using stickers in place of some of the words!

What Is It?

Choose a small, familiar item and put it secretly into a brown lunch bag. Now, describe the item to your child in a clue format that allows your child to guess the contents. Model how to use color words, size words, comparison words, texture words, and more. Then have your child pick an object to place in the bag and let him try to describe the object to you! This is a great way to learn descriptive words and experiment with new vocabulary.

Vacation Challenge!

Splendid Sight Words

Your child is probably already recognizing common sight words, including many of those in the list below. Select a few words at a time to write on index cards and practice. Pick and choose from the list according to your child's interests, the books you are reading, or words you come upon in your daily activities!

Try this fun outdoor activity to combine sight word identification and play:

Sight Word Beanbag Toss. Write 5 to 10 sight words on a driveway or sidewalk with chalk. Draw a chalk circle around each sight word to create a target. Give your child a spot to stand and a beanbag to throw. Every time she tosses a beanbag onto a word, she reads it out loud!

after	does	letter	over	such
again	end	line	page	take
air	even	little	picture	tell
also	follow	live	place	things
America	form	man	play	think
animal	found	me	point	three
another	give	means	put	through
answer	good	men	read	too
any	great	most	right	Try
around	hand	mother	same	turn
ask	help	move	say	Us
away	here	much	sentence	very
back	home	must	set	want
because	house	name	should	well
before	just	need	show	went
big	kind	new	small	where
boy	know	off	sound	why
came	land	old	spell	work
change	large	only	still	world
different	learn	our	study	years

Tips for Summer Math Success

Be positive about math! The more children practice math skills over their vacation, the more prepared they'll be to achieve great things once back in the classroom. Here are some easy ways to integrate mathematics into your child's everyday activities this summer:

- **Play number games during normal daily activities.** For instance, at breakfast you could say, "You had 4 strawberries and 5 blueberries. How many berries is that in all?" Later in the day you might say, "There are 8 toys on the floor. If I pick up 2 of them, how many are left for you to pick up?"

- **Make sure you have at least one analog clock (a clock with hands) in your home.** Ask your child to read the time to you several times each day, starting with time to the hour and half-hour, and gradually moving to the quarter-hour. Eventually you can work on telling time in ten- and five-minute intervals.

- **Keep a calendar somewhere visible, and talk about it each day.** Ask your child what day of the week it is, and how many days are left in the week. Count down the number of days until an upcoming event such as a playdate or trip. Ask him to skip-count by 7 as an extra-hard challenge!

- **Count money all the time!** This is a skill that your child will use every day in life. Keep your change in a small bowl and frequently ask your child to count the contents, or ask her to count the change from your pocket when you're out and about. Be sure to include quarters, dimes, nickels, and pennies. A variation on this is to give your child an amount (example: 14 cents) and have her count out the correct amount of money.

- **Turn car time into math game time.** While you're driving, call out simple addition and subtraction questions and have your child answer them. You can even make word problems—"We've passed three stop signs and will pass two more before we get home. How many stop signs will we pass in total before we get home?"

- **Show how the act of sharing uses simple fractions.** Have your child practice simple fractions by distributing napkins, snacks, or toys equally among family members, and saying what fraction of the items each person received.

Marvelous Math Activities

Lima Bean Addition.

Spray-paint one side of 10 to 20 lima beans, then place between five and ten of the (dry) beans in a small paper cup. To play, have your child shake the beans in the cup and then pour them onto a table. Each bean will show either a natural white surface or a painted one. Ask your child to use the two different colors to show an addition equation on a piece of paper. For example, if one white bean and four red beans were showing, the equation would be 1 + 4 = 5. Return the beans to the cup and repeat the activity.

Pattern Practice.

Using Froot Loops and Cheerios, practice making patterns by stringing different combinations of cereal pieces and colors on string to create a patterned necklace or bracelet. For an extra-sweet, edible treat, use Life Savers on licorice strings.

Sizing Up Shells.

Using a bucket filled with a variety of shells (collected at the beach or purchased from a craft store), ask your child to sort the shells by size—small, medium, and large—or in other ways, like by color or shell shape. You can also encourage your child to measure the shells, pattern the shells, skip count the shells, or use them to make up word problems.

What's Your Sign?

Make a large addition sign and a large subtraction sign out of cardboard. Next, read a simple, one-step word problem out loud and have your child hold up the correct sign as quickly as possible! (Example: "There were two black dogs on the grass. One white dog came to sit with them. How many dogs were on the grass in all?")

Fact Family Race.

An addition/subtraction fact family is a set of three numbers that share four equations. (For example, 2, 3, and 5 are a fact family, because 2 + 3 = 5, 3 + 2 = 5, 5 - 3 = 2, and 5 - 2 = 3.) Write different fact families on a set of index cards. Then challenge your child to select a card and complete the four equations that correspond to that fact family as quickly as possible. When finished with one fact family card, she should move on to a second, a third, and so on. Challenge her to see how many fact families she can complete in five minutes!

Disappearing Act.

On a nice day, take a bucket of water and a paintbrush outside. On a section of dark pavement, use the brush and water to write a math problem or set of problems! Challenge your child to write the answers with the paintbrush before the problems evaporate.

Vacation Challenge!

DIY Estimation Jar

Estimating is an important and useful life skill. Follow these steps to create an estimation jar, and have a blast watching your child's confidence with estimation grow!

1. Find a clear, medium-sized jar made of plastic or glass.
2. Fill the jar with multiples of an item of your choice, such as crayons, erasers, buttons, cotton balls, gummy worms, candy pieces, marbles, or Legos.
3. Let your child examine the closed jar and then estimate the number of objects in the jar. He should write the item and his estimate on a piece of paper.
4. Together, empty the contents of the jar onto a table or other surface. Ask your child to decide "how" to count the items—for example, by ones, by twos, by threes, by fives, or by tens. Talk with him about making that determination based on the size and number of items.
5. Once you've counted the objects together, help your child compare the actual number to his estimate. Was he close? Be sure to record the actual total next to his estimate on the paper for him to keep!

Over the summer, repeat this activity with different objects (or different quantities of the same object). As you change the contents of the jar, refer back to past items and amounts that were in the jar to help your child make more reasonable estimates.

For instance, if the jar is filled with crayons this time but marbles last time, you can talk about the sizes and shapes of those two items. Let that discussion guide your child's estimate for the number of crayons. Does he think there will be more crayons than marbles, or fewer?

Math About Me

Help your child create a "math autobiography" on a large poster board. Write her name in large letters at the top of the board. Then encourage her to think about the different ways numbers are a part of her life, and include them on her poster.
Here are some awesome ideas for Math About Me facts to include:

- I am _____ years old.
- My birthday is on _____.
- I'm in _____ grade in school.
- I am _____ inches tall.
- My shoe size is _____.
- The number of people in my family _____.
- The number of letters in my name is _____.
- The number of pets I have is _____.
- My house number is _____.
- My zip code is _____.
- I wake up at _____.
- I go to bed at _____.
- My favorite number is _____.

- When I was born I weighed _____.
- Now I weigh _____.
- The number of states I've visited is _____.
- I've lost _____ teeth.
- I have _____ rooms in my house.
- My head circumference is _____.
- I am _____ days old.
- An equation that equals my age is _____.
- My phone number is _____.
- The number of cousins I have is __.
- My favorite holiday happens during month number _____.

Your child can simply list "her" math facts on the board, or she can including drawings, stickers, and photos as illustrations. However simple or creative she decides to make it, the most important part is for her to uncover the coolest math facts about herself!

Vacation Challenge!

Hundreds Chart

A hundreds chart is an engaging way to help your child understand and interact with numbers. On the next page are some of the many possible activities you can choose from when using the chart below.

1	2	3	4	5	6	7	8	9	10
11	12	13	14	15	16	17	18	19	20
21	22	23	24	25	26	27	28	29	30
31	32	33	34	35	36	37	38	39	40
41	42	43	44	45	46	47	48	49	50
51	52	53	54	55	56	57	58	59	60
61	62	63	64	65	66	67	68	69	70
71	72	73	74	75	76	77	78	79	80
81	82	83	84	85	86	87	88	89	90
91	92	93	94	95	96	97	98	99	100

- Counting from 1–100

- Learning odd and even numbers

- Developing number sense (what comes before, after, and in between numbers)

- Visualizing patterns of skip counting by 2's, 5's, and 10's

- Addition and "counting on," or subtraction and "counting back"

- **Big Addition.** A hundreds chart is a great way to help your child visualize adding numbers that would normally be TOO BIG for her to handle, such as numbers larger than 10. For example, give your child a problem such as "41 + 25." Have her put a game marker on the first number (41). Then look at the tens digit of the second number ("2" in "25"), and add tens by moving the marker down that many rows on the chart. (From 41, move down 2 rows, going from 41, to 51, to 61.) Next, look at the ones place ("5" in "25") and move the counter to the right five times, counting: 62, 63, 64, 65, 66. This helps children visualize how 41 + 25 = 66.

- **Tens Anywhere.** Practice counting by 10's, but with a twist! Take turns picking a random space on the hundreds chart as a starting spot, and count by 10's to 100. For example, start on 33 and count: 43, 53, 63, 73, 83, 93. As your child grows more confident, try counting by 2's or counting backwards by 10's or 2's.

- **Guess My Number.** While looking at the chart together, give clues that guide your child toward guessing the number you are thinking of! For example, if you are thinking of the number 18, you might say: "I am a two digit number. I am less than 20. I am an even number. The sum of my digits is 9." See how long it takes your child to guess your mystery number!

Game Time!

Beach Bums

This game is endlessly adaptable. Use the suggestions below to mark a set of index cards with skills you'd like your child to practice—or make up your own ideas! Then PICK a skill card set (or SHUFFLE the cards together) to practice. READ the rules. PLAY the game!

- Identify (or write) sight words
- Skip-count by 2's to 20, 5's to 50, or 10's to 100
- Complete all four equations in a fact family
- Say the days of the week in order

- Say the months of the year in order
- Say even (or odd) numbers up to 20
- Roll two number cubes and find the difference
- Clap the syllables in each family member's name

Rules: Two players

1. Place your skill cards in a face-down stack. Place the playing pieces on the Start space.

2. Take turns rolling a number cube and picking a skill card.

3. If you correctly complete the task on the skill card, you can move forward the number of spaces on the number cube.

4. If you land on a space with a number, move the number of spaces in the direction the arrow indicates. If you land on a space with a starfish, take another turn!

The first player to the beach towel wins!

Finish

Hundreds Chart Games

USE the Hundreds Chart on page 120 to play these fun games. USE raisins, pennies, or beans as game markers. READ the rules. PLAY the games!

Race to 100

Rules: Two or more players

1. Start by placing the game markers on the number 1.
2. Each player takes turns rolling two number cubes and finding the sum of the displayed numbers. The player moves his or her marker that many places along the chart.
3. Whichever player is the first to get to 100 wins!

Find the Number Tic-Tac-Toe

Rules: Two players

1. Each player chooses a type of marker (such as raisins for one and beans for the other).
2. Each player takes turns calling out the name of a number on the chart. As they do, the other player finds that number and covers it with his or her marker.
3. As the game progresses with players going back and forth, calling and covering numbers, the chart will fill up with the two marker types.
4. Whichever player is first to get three of their game pieces in a row wins!

We recommend that your child spend at least 20 to 30 minutes each day reading, whether that's reading aloud together with you or reading "on his own" (while you provide support!). Either way, discussing books after you read them helps children absorb the story, think about the messages, and build essential reading comprehension skills. Here are some possible prompts to help get the conversation started.

Fiction

• How did the story make you feel? What did you like or dislike?

• What were you wondering about as you read?

• Does this story make you think of anything else you've read?

• What was your favorite page and why?

• Were there any parts that surprised you?

• Which character from the story would you want as a friend and why?

• Describe the setting in the story (time and place).

• In your opinion, what was the most important part of the story?

• Choose one character. Explain two character traits that describe him or her.

• If you could change the end of the story, how would you change it?

Nonfiction

• What is the main topic of the book? What is it mostly about?

• What are two new facts you learned from the book?

• What is the title of the book? Make up a new title.

• How do the photographs, charts, or diagrams in the book help you while reading?

• What questions do you still have after reading the book?

• Why do you think the author chose to write about this topic?

• How can learning about this topic help you in the world?

• Who would you recommend this book to and why?

• What were you wondering about as you read the book?

• Would this be a topic you would want to learn more about? Why or why not?

Recommended Reading List

Kids this age love reading books that are part of a series! Revisiting favorite characters and familiar situations helps make the reading experience both enjoyable and successful. These suggested series contain books that are "just right" for children practicing reading to themselves.

Fly Guy (Tedd Arnold)

Biscuit (Alyssa Satin Capucilli)

Max Spaniel (David Catrow)

Now I'm Reading! Levels 1-4
(Nora Gaydos)

Danny and the Dinosaur (Syd Hoff)

Boris on the Move (Andrew Joyner)

Pete the Cat (Eric Litwin)

Frog and Toad (Arnold Lobel)

Little Critter (Mercer Mayer)

Little Bear (Else Holmelund Minarik)

Mr. Putter & Tabby (Cynthia Rylant)

Poppleton (Cynthia Rylant)

Nate the Great
(Marjorie Weinman Sharmat)

Rabbit & Robot (Andrew Smith)

Noodles (Hans Wilhelm)

Elephant & Piggie (Mo Willems)

Morris the Moose (Bernard Wiseman)

When helping your child select a "just right" book, consider the following:

Too Easy
- No tricky words
- I can read without thinking
- I can read it very quickly

Too Hard
- More than 5 tricky words on a page
- I can't remember what I read
- I read without expression

Just Right
- Fewer than 5 tricky words on a page
- I think about the story as I read
- I read at my own pace
- I read the words with expression
- I enjoy the experience of reading

You're the Critic

Pick some of your favorite (or least favorite) books and write a review for each. Color in the number of stars you'd give each book!

Book 1 Title:

Book 1 Author:

My Review: ☆☆☆☆

Book 2 Title:

Book 2 Author:

My Review: ☆☆☆☆

Book 3 Title:

Book 3 Author:

My Review: ☆☆☆☆

Remarkable Reads

Recommended Math Reading List

Did you know? Books don't "just" help children develop their reading ability—they can also be a great way to reinforce math concepts such as number and shape recognition. Here are some fantastic reads that help develop math skills.

Math Chapter Books to Explore

7 x 9 = Trouble! by Claudia Mills

Fractions = Trouble! by Claudia Mills

Ben Franklin and the Magic Squares by Frank Murphy

How Big Is a Foot? by Rolf Myller

How Many Guinea Pigs Can Fit on a Plane? by Laura Overdeck

Math Picture Books to Investigate

Place Value by David A. Adler

Triangle by Mac Barnett

365 Penguins by Jean-Luc Fromental

Equal Shmequal by Virginia Kroll

Seeing Symmetry by Loreen Leedy

Inch by Inch by Leo Lionni

Bean Thirteen by Matthew McElligott

Lemonade for Sale by Stuart J. Murphy

One Hundred Hungry Ants by Elinor J. Pinczes

If You Were a Minus Sign by Trisha Speed Shaskan

You're the Critic

Pick some of your favorite (or least favorite) books and write a review for each. Color in the number of stars you'd give each book!

Book 1 Title:

Book 1 Author:

My Review: ☆☆☆☆

Book 2 Title:

Book 2 Author:

My Review: ☆☆☆☆

Book 3 Title:

Book 3 Author:

My Review: ☆☆☆☆

Answers

Page 2
1. bike
2. bed
3. fish
4. goat
5. dog
6. desk
7. bus
8. fork
9. doll
10. gum

Page 3

Page 4
1. quick, quit
2. jeans, jam
3. kite, kick
4. hand
5. keep

Page 5
1. hand
2. king
3. queen
4. jar
5. kite
6. quilt
7. hat
8. jug

Page 6
l: leaf, log
m: mat, mop
n: nose, net
p: pan, pig

Page 7

Page 8
1. tent
2. ring
3. tooth
4. rooster
5. tomato
6. seal
7. six
8. red
9. tub
10. saw

Page 9

rake
sun
rose
tape
tooth
sink
top
rock
tie
sock
rug
seal

Page 10
v: van, vase
w: wig, web
y: yellow, yo-yo
z: zipper, zebra

Page 11

v   es   wi
an   v   t   ng
x-ay   rn ze
r   ya   ro

1. van
2. vest
3. wing
4. x-ray
5. yarn
6. zero

Page 12
1. red
2. sub
3. mop
4. drum
5. fan
6. hand
7. crib
8. ram
9. top
10. moon

Page 13
1. gum, clam
2. moon
3. food, sad
4. jump, top
5. rub

Page 14

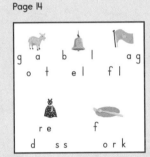

g   a   b   l   a g
o   t   el   f l
re   f
d   ss   o r k

1. goat
2. bell
3. flag
4. dress
5. fork

Page 15

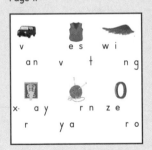

nut
bag
nail
duck
bus
net
shell
clock
gift
doll
gas
pig

Page 16
1. mitten
2. seven
3. pillow
4. pizza
5. zipper
6. robot
7. lemon
8. kitten
9. ladder
10. raccoon

Page 17
1. metal
2. jacket
3. hammer
4. jelly
5. wagon

Page 18
1. thumb
2. truck
3. chair
4. shoe
5. shirt
6. ship
7. shark
8. tree
9. thimble
10. cheese

Page 19
1. splash
2. moth
3. beach
4. brush
5. bench

Page 20

Answers

Page 21

Page 22
1. bed
2. nest
3. sled
4. net
5. web
6. pen

Page 23
1. nest
2. egg
3. ten
4. web
5. bed

Page 24

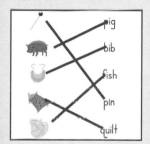

pig
bib
fish
pin
quilt

Page 25
1. dish, wish
2. pit
3. bib
4. hig, wig
5. mix

Page 26

Page 27

Page 28
1. plug
2. rug
3. bus
4. sun
5. mud
6. tub

Page 29
1. rug
2. cup
3. sub
4. gum
5. truck

Page 30

Page 31

Page 32
1. tree
2. knee
3. queen
4. bee
5. green
6. sheep

Page 33
1. bee
2. green
3. wheel
4. three
5. heel

Page 34

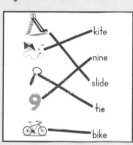

kite
nine
slide
tie
bike

Page 35
1. bite
2. hive
3. tie
4. wipe, ripe
5. fine, dine

Page 36

Page 37

Page 38
1. blue
2. flute
3. tube
4. mule
5. cube
6. glue

Page 39
1. mule
2. cube
3. flute
4. glue
5. blue

Page 40
1. cupcake
2. starfish
3. doorbell
4. raincoat
5. ladybug

Page 41
1. doghouse
2. snowman
3. catfish
4. football
5. rainbow

Answers

Page 42
1. din|ner, din, ner
2. kit|ten, kit, ten
3. mit|ten, mit, ten
4. hap|pen, hap, pen
5. pup|pet, pup, pet
6. zip|per, zip, per
7. muf|fin, muf, fin
8. but|ton, but, ton

Page 43
1. ple
2. mer
3. ten
4. za
5. py
6. low

Page 44
1. nap|kin, nap, kin
2. bas|ket, bas, ket
3. doc|tor, doc, tor
4. pic|nic, pic, nic
5. mon|key, mon, key
6. win|ter, win, ter
7. sis|ter, sis, ter
8. pen|cil, pen, cil

Page 45
1. wal
2. tur
3. tur
4. roos
5. mon
6. pen

Page 46
Fruits: lemon, apple, orange, grapes
Vegetables: corn, carrot, broccoli, lettuce

Page 47
1. olive
2. dog
3. yarn

Page 48
Summer clothes: shorts, sandals, swimsuit
Winter clothes: earmuffs, scarf, mittens

Page 49
1. five
2. zebra
3. bat

Page 50

Page 51
A Special Cake

Page 52
3 Mom waters the garden.
2 Kate and Tim plant the seeds.
1 Dad digs up the dirt.

Page 53
1 Grandma and Juan stop at the baker's.
3 Juan eats a peach.
2 Grandma buys some flowers.

Page 54

Page 55

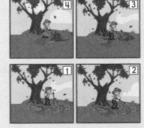

Page 56
1. b
2. a
3. b

Page 57
Suggestion: a puppy

Page 58
a. Milk the cow and feed the chickens and pigs

Page 60

Page 61

Page 62

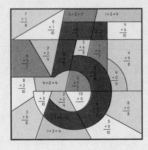

Page 63
1. 7   2. 6
3. 5   4. 2
5. 9   6. 8
Combination: 2 5 6 7 8 9

Page 64
Have someone check your answers.

Page 65
1. 4   2. 10
3. 9   4. 6
5. 8   6. 1
7. 5   8. 7
9. 3
BECAUSE 7 8 9!

Page 66

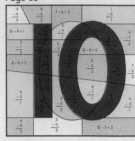

Page 67
1. 2   2. 4
3. 3   4. 8
5. 6   6. 0
Combination: 8 6 4 3 2 0

Page 68

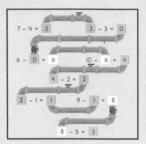

Page 69
8 + 1 = 9
1 + 8 = 9
9 – 8 = 1
9 – 1 = 8

5 + 4 = 9
4 + 5 = 9
9 – 5 = 4
9 – 4 = 5

6 + 3 = 9
3 + 6 = 9
9 – 6 = 3
9 – 3 = 6

Page 70

Page 71

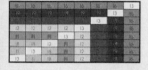

Page 72

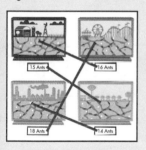

Page 73

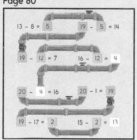

Page 74
1. 15   2. 20
3. 12   4. 11
5. 18   6. 14
Combination: 11 12 14 15 18 20

Page 75
1. 13   2. 19
3. 11   4. 15
5. 18   6. 20
7. 14   8. 12
9. 16
AT THE MOOVIES!

Page 76
Have someone check
your answers.

Page 77

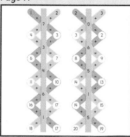

Page 78
1. 8   2. 11
3. 2   4. 9
5. 15   6. 3

Page 79
1. 12   2. 6
3. 9   4. 18
5. 5   6. 1
Combination: 18 12 9 6 5 1

Page 80

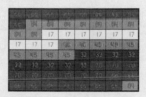

Page 81
$11 + 6 = 17$
$6 + 11 = 17$
$17 - 11 = 6$
$17 - 6 = 11$

$15 + 2 = 17$
$2 + 15 = 17$
$17 - 15 = 2$
$17 - 2 = 15$

$14 + 3 = 17$
$3 + 14 = 17$
$17 - 14 = 3$
$17 - 3 = 14$

Pages 82-83

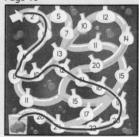

Pages 84-85
THE SECRET PLANS ARE HIDDEN
IN THE VASE ON THE DESK.

Page 86

Page 87
1. 43   2. 18
3. 52   4. 61
5. 36   6. 29
Combination: 6 5 4 3 2 1

Page 88
1. 429   2. 517
3. 392   4. 681
5. 168   6. 732

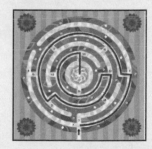

Page 89
1. 238   2. 714
3. 452   4. 521
5. 946   6. 187
A PARRRTY HAT.

Page 90

Page 91
Have someone check
your answers

Page 92

Answers

Page 93

Page 94
Have someone check your answers.

Page 95

Page 96
Have someone check your answers.

Page 97
1. 13   2. 9

Page 98

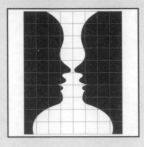

Page 99

Page 100
Have someone check your answers.

Page 101

Page 102

4 :00

Page 103

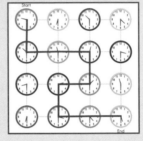

Page 104

Page 105

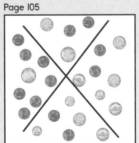

Page 106
1. 1¢   2. 25¢
3. 5¢   4. 11¢
5. 20¢   6. 15¢
7. 36¢   8. 17¢
IN A SNOW BANK!

Page 107

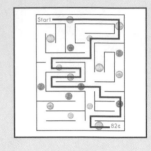

Page 108

I'M SUMMER SMART!

This award is presented to

_____

on _____

for a great job finishing the
**Sylvan Summer Smart:
Between Grades
1 & 2 Workbook!**

Sylvan
Learning℠

Sylvan Learning℠

STAY SHARP FOR SCHOOL!

New from America's #1 Tutoring Brand!

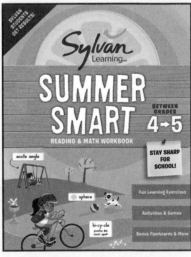

Additional workbooks and flash cards available wherever children's books are sold.

RHCBooks.com   RHCB

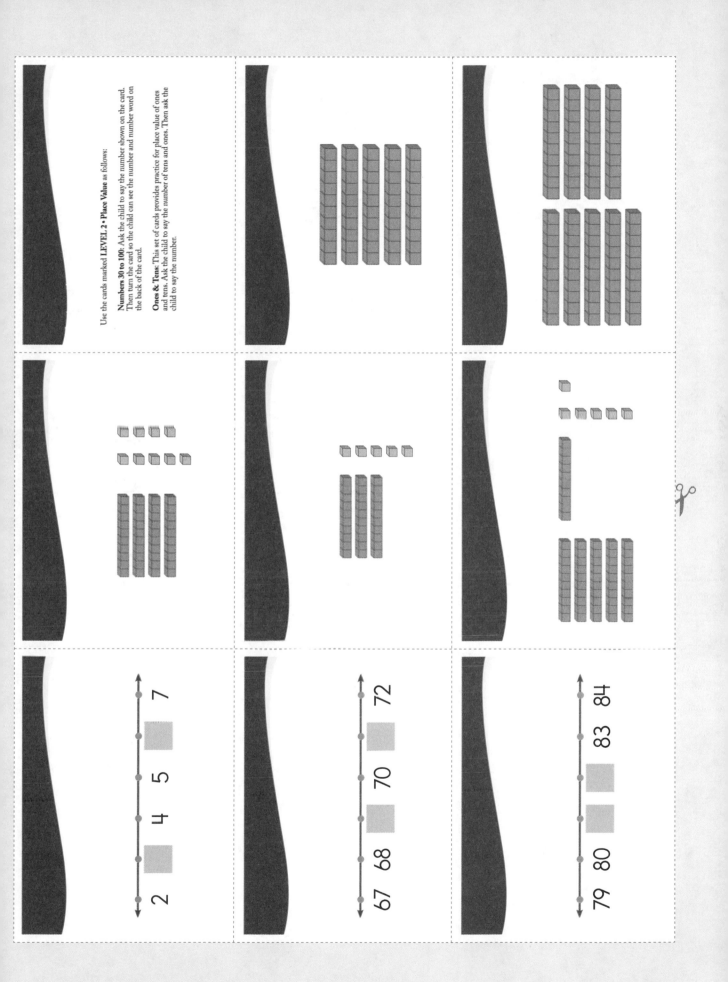

Use the cards marked **LEVEL 2 • Place Value** as follows:

Numbers 30 to 100: Ask the child to say the number shown on the card. Then turn the card so the child can see the number and number word on the back of the card.

Ones & Tens: This set of cards provides practice for place value of ones and tens. Ask the child to say the number of tens and ones. Then ask the child to say the number.

2 4 5

7

67 68 70

72

79 80 83 84

137

Ones, Tens & Hundreds: This set of cards provides practice for place value of ones, tens, and hundreds. Ask the child to say the number of hundreds, tens, and ones. Then ask the child to say the number.

Place Value

Tens	Ones
4	9	= 49

Place Value—Ones & Tens

Number Patterns—Number Lines

2 3 4 5 6 7

Place Value—Numbers 30 to 100

50

fifty

Place Value—Ones & Tens

Tens	Ones
3	5	= 35

Number Patterns—Number Lines

67 68 69 70 71 72

Place Value—Numbers 30 to 100

90

ninety

Place Value—Ones & Tens

Tens	Ones
6	6	= 66

Number Patterns—Number Lines

79 80 81 82 83 84

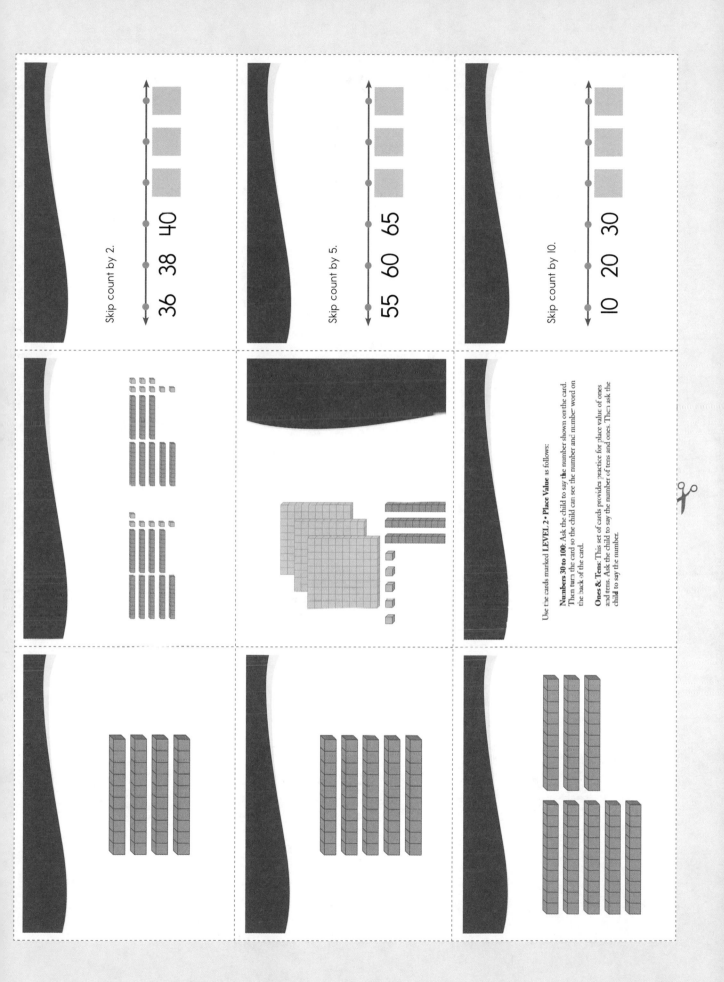

Skip count by 2.

36 38 40

Skip count by 5.

55 60 65

Skip count by 10.

10 20 30

Use the cards marked **LEVEL 2 • Place Value** as follows:

Numbers 30 to 100: Ask the child to say the number shown on the card. Then turn the card so the child can see the number and number word on the back of the card.

Ones & Tens: This set of cards provides practice for place value of ones and tens. Ask the child to say the number of tens and ones. Then ask the child to say the number.

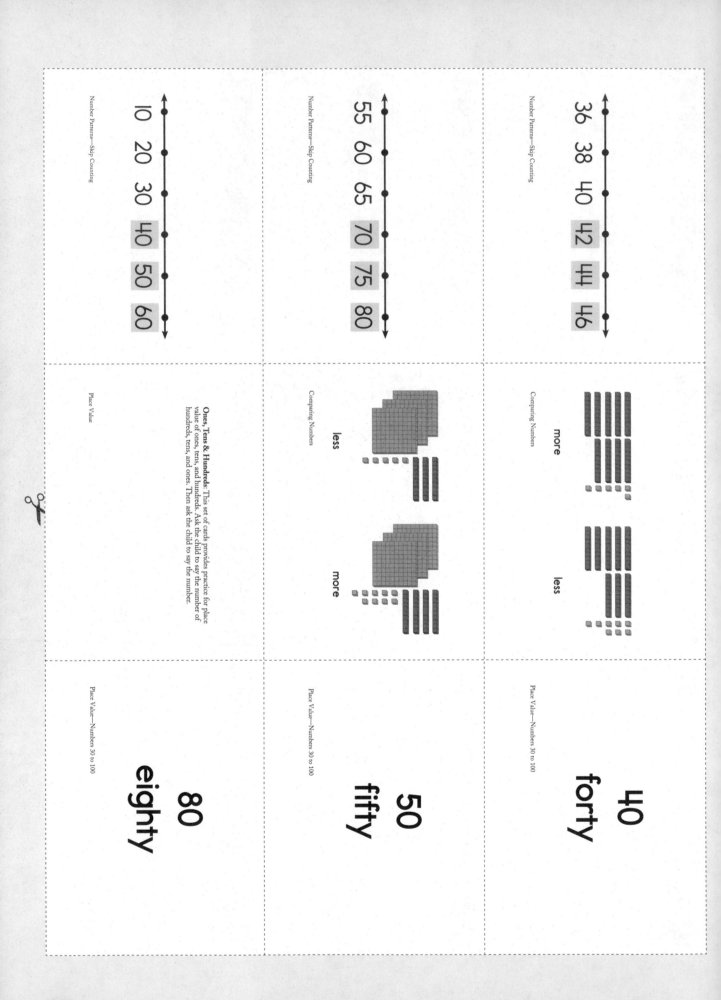

Number Patterns—Skip Counting

36 38 40 42 44 46

Number Patterns—Skip Counting

55 60 65 70 75 80

Number Patterns—Skip Counting

10 20 30 40 50 60

Comparing Numbers

more

less

Comparing Numbers

less

more

Ones, Tens & Hundreds: This set of cards provides practice for place value of ones, tens, and hundreds. Ask the child to say the number of hundreds, tens, and ones. Then ask the child to say the number.

Place Value

Place Value—Numbers 30 to 100

40
forty

Place Value—Numbers 30 to 100

50
fifty

Place Value—Numbers 30 to 100

80
eighty

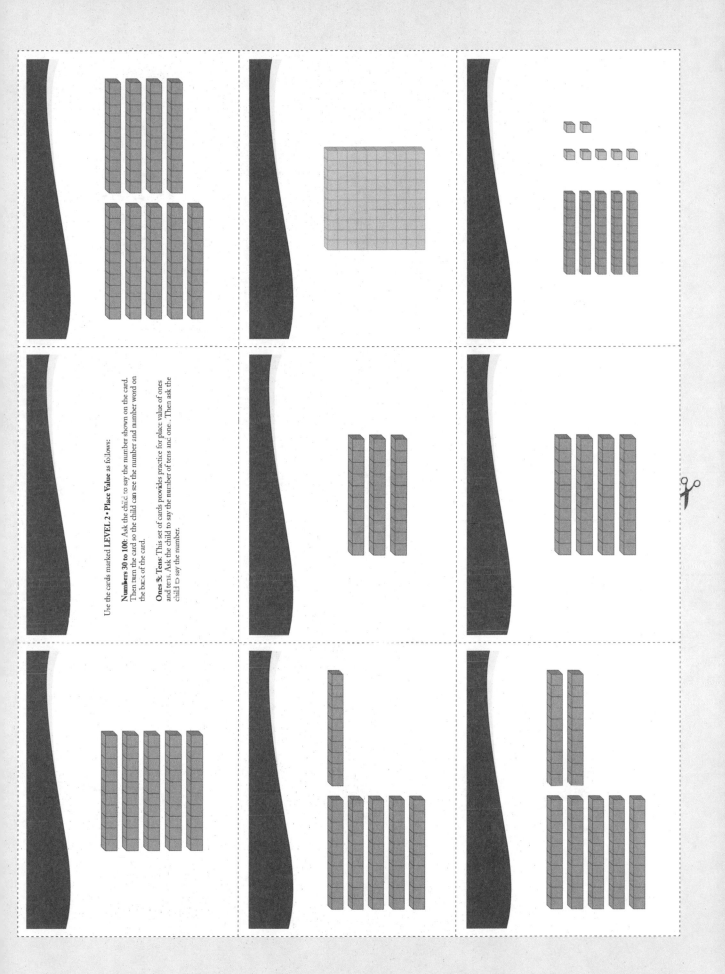

Use the cards marked **LEVEL 2 • Place Value** as follows:

Numbers 30 to 100: Ask the child to say the number shown on the card. Then turn the card so the child can see the number and number word on the back of the card.

Ones & Tens: This set of cards provides practice for place value of ones and tens. Ask the child to say the number of tens and ones. Then ask the child to say the number.

141

Tens	Ones
5	7

5 7 = 57

100
one hundred

90
ninety

Ones, Tens & Hundreds: This set of cards provides practice for place value of ones, tens, and hundreds. Ask the child to say the number of hundreds, tens, and ones. Then ask the child to say the number.

40
forty

30
thirty

50
fifty

70
seventy

60
sixty

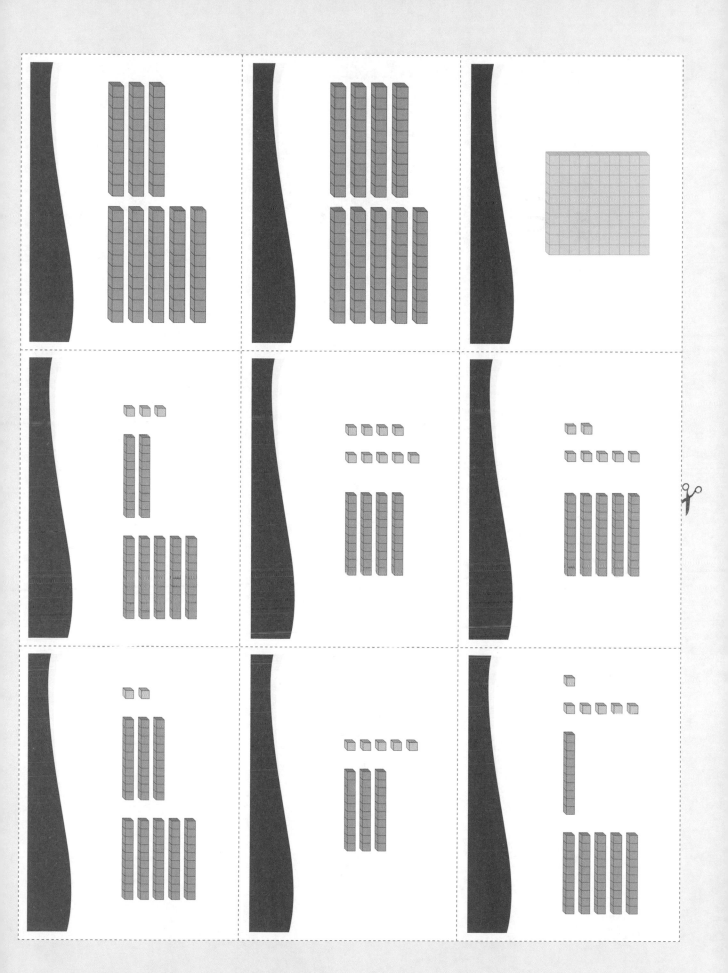

143

80
eighty

90
ninety

100
one hundred

Tens	Ones
7	3

= 73

Tens	Ones
4	9

= 49

Tens	Ones
5	7

= 57

Tens	Ones
8	2

= 82

Tens	Ones
3	5

= 35

Tens	Ones
6	6

= 66

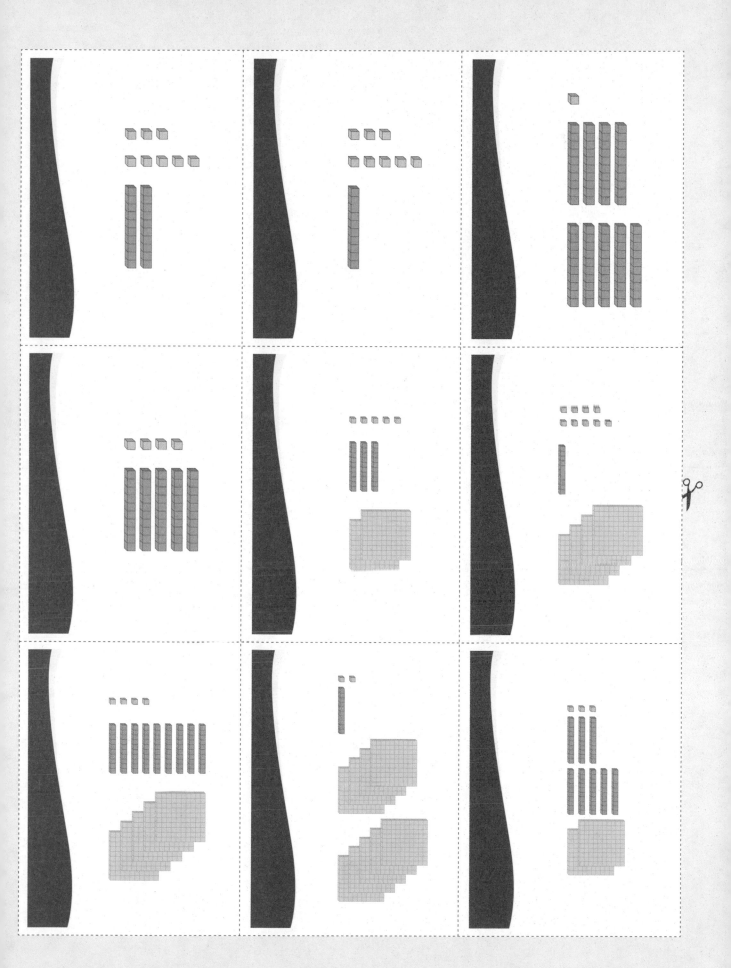

Tens	Ones
2	8

= 28

Tens	Ones
5	4

= 54

Hundreds	Tens	Ones
5	9	4

= 594

Tens	Ones
1	8

= 18

Hundreds	Tens	Ones
2	3	5

= 235

Hundreds	Tens	Ones
9	1	2

= 912

Tens	Ones
9	1

= 91

Hundreds	Tens	Ones
4	1	9

= 419

Hundreds	Tens	Ones
2	8	3

= 283

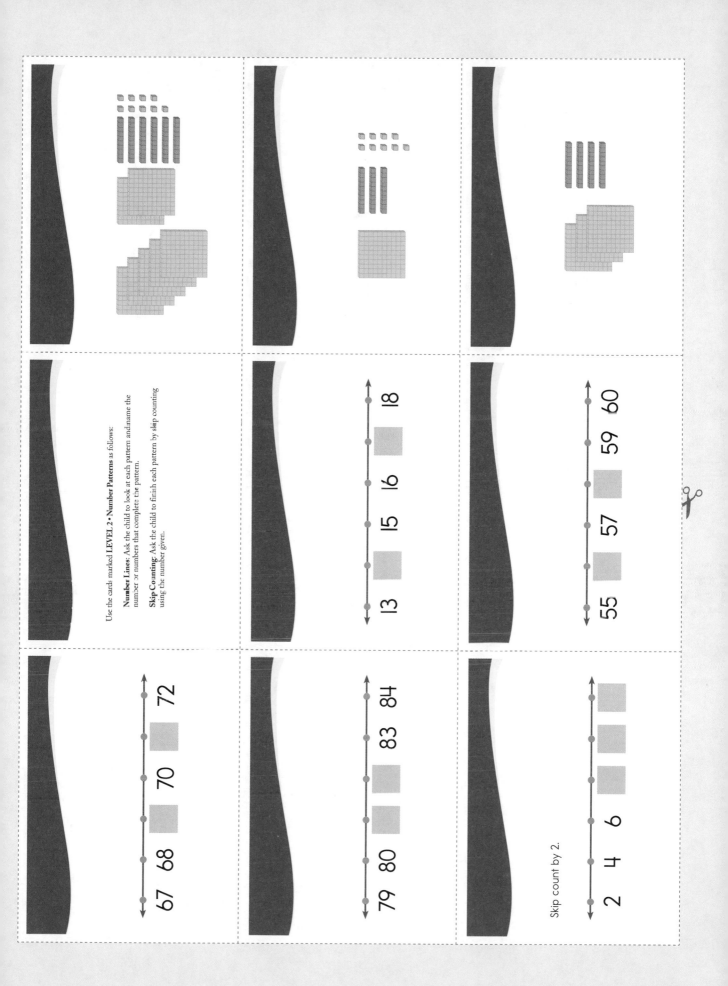

Use the cards marked **LEVEL 2 • Number Patterns** as follows:

Number Lines: Ask the child to look at each pattern and name the number or numbers that complete the pattern.

Skip Counting: Ask the child to finish each pattern by skip counting using the number given.

13   15 16   18

55   57   59 60

67 68   70   72

79 80   83 84

Skip count by 2.

2   4   6

Place Value—Ones, Tens & Hundreds

Hundreds	Tens	Ones
7	6	9

= 769

Place Value—Ones, Tens & Hundreds

Hundreds	Tens	Ones
1	3	9

= 139

Place Value—Ones, Tens & Hundreds

Hundreds	Tens	Ones
3	4	0

= 340

Number Patterns

Number Patterns—Number Lines

13 14 15 16 17 18

Number Patterns—Number Lines

67 68 69 70 71 72

Number Patterns—Number Lines

79 80 81 82 83 84

Number Patterns—Number Lines

55 56 57 58 59 60

Number Patterns—Skip Counting

2 4 6 8 10 12

148

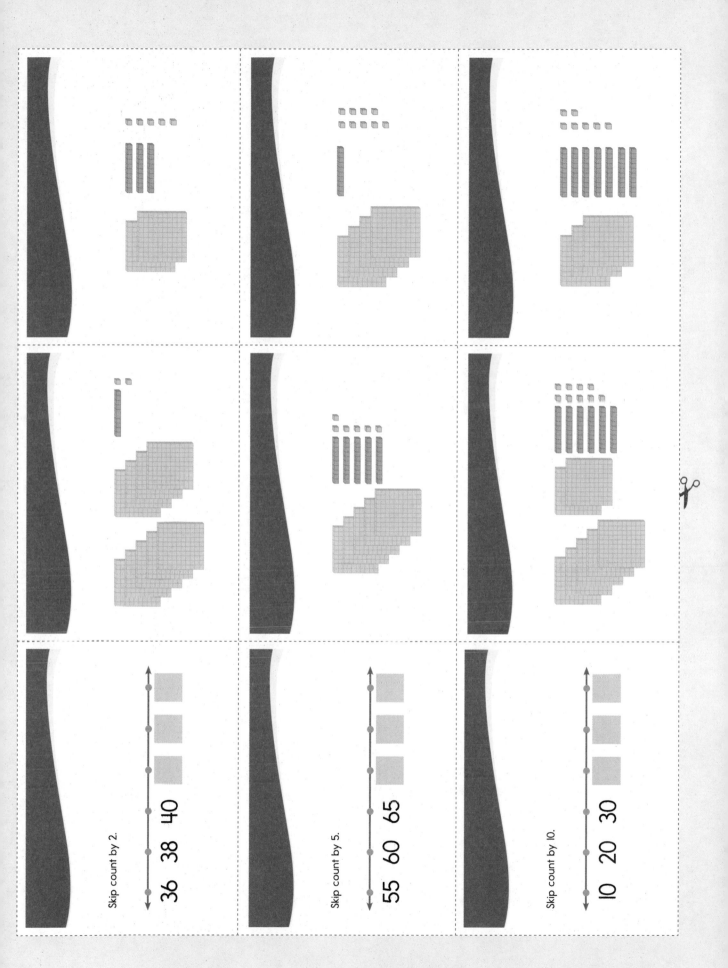

Skip count by 2.

36 38 40

Skip count by 5.

55 60 65

Skip count by 10.

10 20 30

149

Place Value—Ones, Tens & Hundreds

Hundreds	Tens	Ones
2	3	5

= 235

Place Value—Ones, Tens & Hundreds

Hundreds	Tens	Ones
4	1	9

= 419

Place Value—Ones, Tens & Hundreds

Hundreds	Tens	Ones
3	7	7

= 377

Place Value—Ones, Tens & Hundreds

Hundreds	Tens	Ones
9	1	2

= 912

Place Value—Ones, Tens & Hundreds

Hundreds	Tens	Ones
5	5	6

= 556

Place Value—Ones, Tens & Hundreds

Hundreds	Tens	Ones
7	6	9

= 769

Number Patterns—Skip Counting

36 38 40 42 44 46

Number Patterns—Skip Counting

55 60 65 70 75 80

Number Patterns—Skip Counting

10 20 30 40 50 60

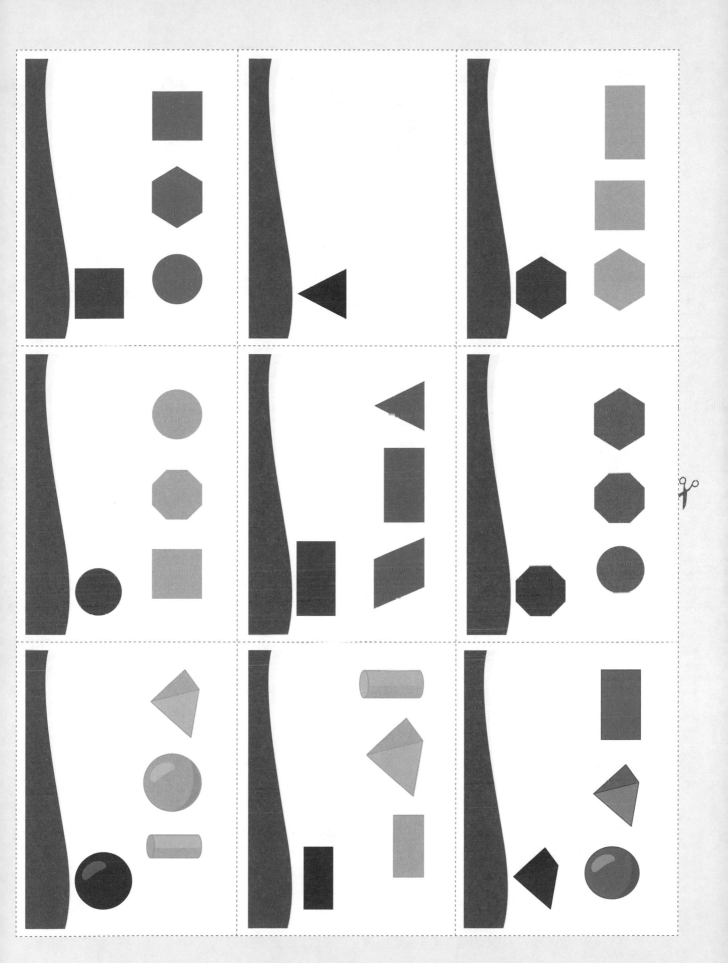

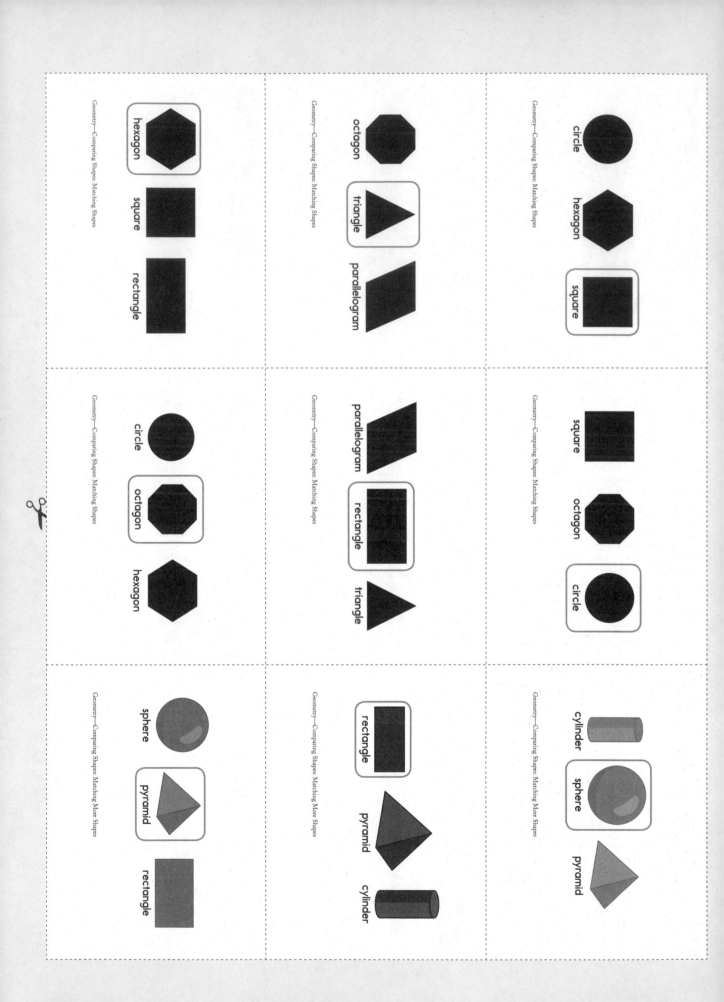

circle hexagon square

square octagon circle

cylinder sphere pyramid

octagon triangle parallelogram

parallelogram rectangle triangle

rectangle pyramid cylinder

hexagon square rectangle

circle octagon hexagon

sphere pyramid rectangle

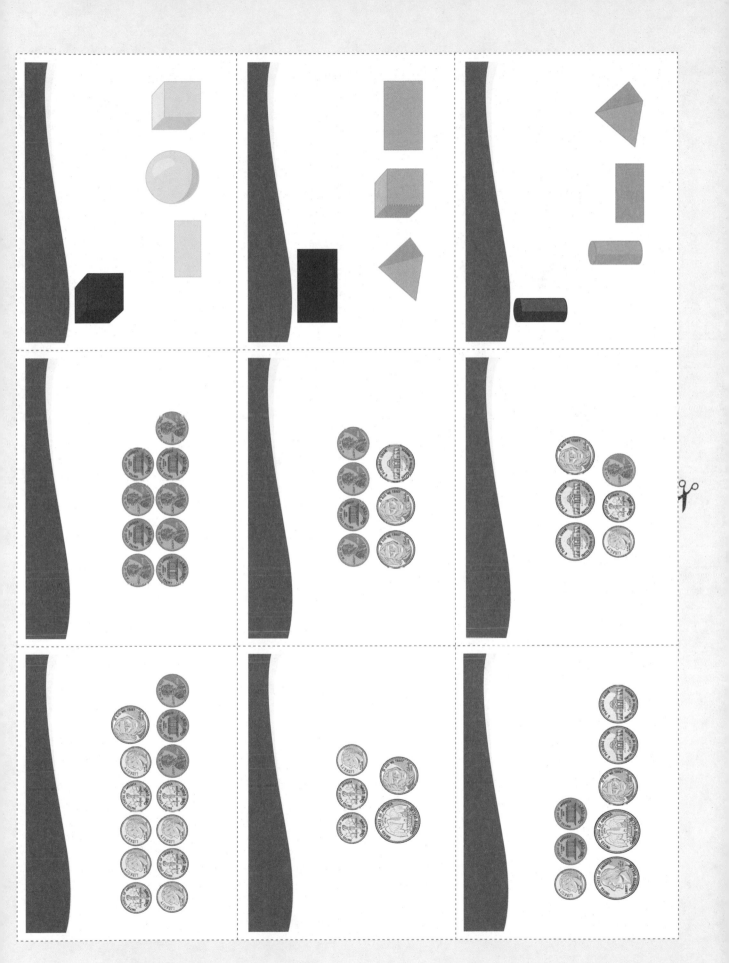

153

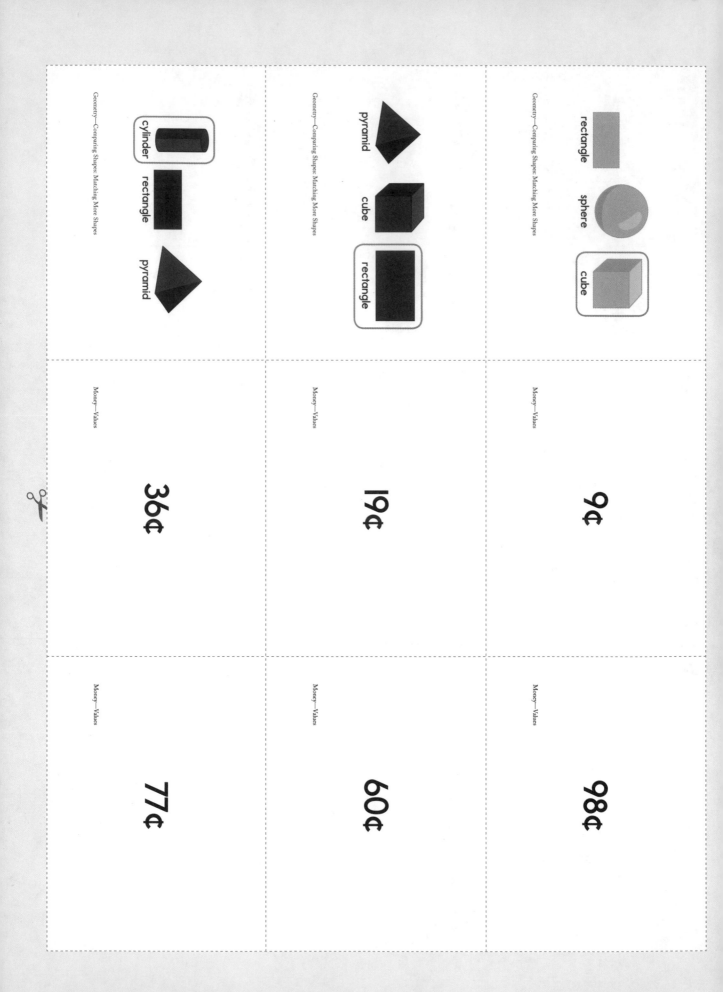

rectangle

sphere

cube

Geometry—Comparing Shapes: Matching More Shapes

pyramid

cube

rectangle

Geometry—Comparing Shapes: Matching More Shapes

cylinder

rectangle

pyramid

Geometry—Comparing Shapes: Matching More Shapes

Money—Values

9¢

Money—Values

19¢

Money—Values

36¢

Money—Values

98¢

Money—Values

60¢

Money—Values

77¢